The Body
Dynamic

The Body
Dynamic

John MacArthur, Jr.

ChariotVICTOR
PUBLISHING
A DIVISION OF COOK COMMUNICATIONS

Victor Books is an imprint of ChariotVictor Publishing,
a division of Cook Communications, Colorado Springs, Colorado 80918
Cook Communications, Paris, Ontario
Kingsway Communications, Eastbourne, England

Editors: Jerry Yamamoto; Barbara Williams

Design: Andrea Boven

Cover Photo: Photonica—Eric Perry

ISBN:1-56476-586-5

Suggested Subject Heading: BIBLE STUDY

1 2 3 4 5 6 7 8 9 10 Printing/Year 00 99 98 97 96

Contents

Introduction

What is the church? Many conceive it to be anything from well-structured, wealthy, highly organized institutions to underground cell groups with no money or structure. But what is the biblical description of the church? How do we express its identity and fulfill Christ's desire for it? Perhaps the following description of Christians attributed to Aristides, a second-century secular philosopher, provides the truest definition of what the church ought to be:

> They abstain from all impurity, in the hope of the recompense that is to come in another world. As for their servants or handmaids or children, they persuade them to become Christians by the love they have for them; and when they have become so, they call them without distinction, brothers. They do not worship strange gods; and they walk in all humility and kindness and falsehood is not found among them and they love one another. When they see the stranger they bring him to their homes and rejoice over him as over a true brother; for they do not call brothers those who are after the flesh, but those who are in the Spirit and in God.

> And there is among them a man that is poor and needy and if they have not an abundance of necessities, they fast two or three days that they may supply the needy with the necessary food.

> They observe scrupulously the commandment of their Messiah; they live honestly and soberly as the Lord their God commanded

them. Every morning and all hours on account of the goodness of God toward them, they praise and laud Him and over their food and their drink, they render Him thanks.

And if any righteous person of their number passes away from this world, they rejoice and give thanks to God and they follow his body as though he were moving from one place to another. And when a child is born to them, they praise God, and if again it chances to die in its infancy, they praise God mightily, as for one who has passed through the world without sins.

Such is the law of the Christians and such is their conduct ("The Apology of Aristides," *Encyclopedia Britannica*, vol. 1, [1929 edition], p. 346).

Aristides made no mention of a building, or an organization, or even specific leaders. He saw the church simply as individual people functioning as one group, ministering to and caring for one another. That is truly what the church is.

Another way to describe the church is to use a compelling metaphor. The New Testament does that by using various metaphors for the church that the Old Testament also uses for Israel. They are both called a bride, or wife (Hosea 1:2; cf. Jer. 3:20; Rev. 21:2); a family household (Ps. 107:41; Jer. 31:1; Eph. 2); a flock (Isa. 40:11; cf. Ps. 23; Luke 12:32; Acts 20:28-29); and a vineyard or vine branches (Isa. 5:1-7; John 15:5).

But one metaphor is unique to the New Testament, and that is the metaphor that speaks of the church as Christ's Body. That reveals the church not as an organization but as a living organism made up of many interrelated and mutually dependent parts. Christ is the head of this Body, and the Holy Spirit is, as it were, its lifeblood. This unique metaphor forms the basis of this book.

Two of the Apostle Paul's epistles provide the most comprehensive instruction about the Body of Christ: Ephesians and 1 Corinthians. We will examine the key passages out of those letters, in addition to several other important passages.

The metaphor of the Body of Christ runs throughout the Book

of Ephesians, beginning with its opening chapter, where Paul looks into the past to view the divine plan of the church. There we find that God the Father, Son, and Holy Spirit all had a part in the planning of the church. That will be the focus of the first chapter.

In the next three chapters we will see how the formation of the Body of Christ in eternity past lays a foundation on which the Christian can build a life that will honor God. In chapter 2 we will specifically examine the resources available to every believer. In chapter 3 we will see how each Christian gains entrance into the Body through God's salvation plan. And in chapter 4 we'll learn about the power God has made available to all believers to help them live the life God has designed for them.

The remaining chapters form the second section of the book, which deals with how the Body of Christ should work in the world. Chapter 5 will continue with our analysis of Ephesians, in particular how each believer should act in the Body. Then in chapter 6 we will look at how the leadership of the church helps the Body grow toward maturity.

With chapter 7 we'll take our first look at 1 Corinthians 12 and deal with the theme of the Body's unity. Chapter 8 will analyze the gifts of the Body, as we'll see how each member has been uniquely gifted by God.

Chapters 9 and 10 will bring our look at this unique body metaphor to a close. We'll see the importance of fellowship among the members of the Body and, perhaps most important, how the Body is to serve as a witness of Christ to the world.

God has provided us with a clear blueprint of how the Body of Christ is to work in the world. But that plan is useless and unfulfilled unless you and I make it part of our lives. My prayer is that as you study and apply the principles you learn in this book, you'll become an effective and key member of the church, the Body of Christ.

Part 1
The Church:
The Body of Christ

1

The Formation
of the Body

The Body of Christ transcends place and time. The sovereign design of Almighty God formed it in the timelessness of eternity. The Apostle Paul writes that God has "made known to us the mystery [sacred secret, hidden in the Old Testament] of His will . . . with a view to an administration suitable to the fulness of the times, that is, the summing up of all things in Christ" (Eph. 1:9-10). "That by revelation there was made known to me the mystery. . . . Which in other generations was not made known to the sons of men, as it has now been revealed to His holy apostles and prophets in the Spirit" (3:3, 5).

Then Paul explains "that the Gentiles are fellow-heirs and fellow-members of the body" (v. 6). His mission, he goes on to say, is "to bring to light what is the administration of the mystery" (v. 9). This is the mystery of the Body: Jew and Gentile have been gathered together and molded into a single Body, of which Christ is the head. God is forming a Body of Jew and Gentile, rich and poor, learned and unlearned, male and female, slave and free—"one new man" (2:15).

A mystery in the biblical sense is a truth God ordained in eternity past and hid, to be revealed at a certain time. Before any of us were born, before the earth was formed, God planned the Body of Christ (1:3-6). Paul thus ascribes the forming of the mystery Body to eternity past.

To realize that God loved me and placed me within the Body of Christ, before the world was even created, is cause for rejoicing.

Contemplating that truth caused Paul to burst out in a great song of praise in Ephesians 1:3-14, which is one sentence of 200 words in the Greek, and may be the longest sentence in religious literature. It is connected, yet disconnected, and since it is a complicated sentence, we must study it piece by piece.

This lyrical song of praise flows from Paul's heart. His mind goes from glory to glory, from gift to gift, from wonder to wonder. He discusses election, sanctification, foreordination, identification, adoption, acceptance, redemption, sanctification, enrichment, enlightenment, glorification, inheritance, and the sealing of the Holy Spirit. All the cardinal doctrines are included in his song of praise as the apostle reviews how God formed the Body before the world began.

Paul constantly gives God the glory: "to the praise of the glory of His grace" (v. 6); "that we . . . should be to the praise of His glory" (v. 12); "to the praise of His glory" (v. 14). His song of praise actually has three parts: first, the past aspect of God's eternal formation of the Body (vv. 4-6); followed by the present (vv. 6-11); and the future (vv. 12-14). Thus God's eternal plan for the Body has three parts: the past—election; the present—redemption; the future—inheritance.

As Paul dwells on God's formation of the Body in eternity past (vv. 4-6), he presents seven facts. He reveals the method by which the Body was elected; the objects of God's election; the time of election; the purpose of the Body; the motive for God's election; the result of His election; and the goal of the Body.

The Method of Election

Paul describes the method when he says, "He chose us in Him" (Eph. 1:4). God didn't draw straws; by His sovereign will He chose who would be in the Body of Christ. The Greek root for "chosen" is *eklego*, which means "to call out" or "to elect." God made His choice totally apart from human will and purely on the basis of His sovereignty. Since the Greek verb for "chosen" is in the middle voice and thus reflexive, the meaning is: "according as He has chosen us for Himself." God acted totally independent of any outside influence. Paul's heart overflowed at such a glorious thought as he blessed God for choosing unworthy sinners.

God wrote the names of every believer in the Book of Life before the world began: "The beast that you saw was and is not, and is about to come up out of the abyss and to go to destruction. And those who dwell on the earth will wonder, whose name has not been written in the book of life from the foundation of the world" (Rev. 17:8; see also 20:15).

Election is the first cause of all blessing. That is why Paul begins with it in Ephesians 1:4. In Scripture, God does everything according to His own will and mind. Israel was elect (Ex. 6). The angels were elect (1 Tim. 5:21). Christ was elect (1 Peter 2:6). Certain believers were elected for certain tasks (Acts 9:15). The forming of the Body is therefore by God's choice.

Jesus said to His disciples, "You did not choose Me, but I chose you, and appointed you" (John 15:16). And in the same Gospel, John said, "But as many as received Him, to them He gave the right to become children of God, even to those who believe in His name: who were born not of blood, nor of the will of the flesh, nor of the will of man, but of God" (1:12-13).

Paul reiterated the election of God in his other epistles: "Who has saved us, and called us with a holy calling, not according to our works, but according to His own purpose and grace which was granted us in Christ Jesus from all eternity" (2 Tim. 1:9). "For this reason I endure all things for the sake of those who are chosen, that they also may obtain the salvation which is in Christ Jesus and with it eternal glory" (2:10). "But we should always give thanks to God for you, brethren beloved by the Lord, because God has chosen you from the beginning for salvation" (2 Thes. 2:13).

Rest assured, these statements defining God's sovereign election of believers are not in the Bible to cause controversy. Election is a fact that does not exclude human responsibility or people's personal response by faith. Jesus said, "The one who comes to Me I will certainly not cast out" (John 6:37). Admittedly the two concepts of God's sovereignty and human responsibility don't seem to go together. However, both are true separately, and we must accept by faith that paradox. But there is no paradox in the mind of God. Our faith and salvation rest entirely on God's election of us, and yet the day a person comes to Jesus Christ, that person comes because he or she desires to. Yet even that desire is given to us by God, and He supplies the necessary faith so we can believe. If salvation depends on us, then praise to God is ridiculous. But, in truth, our praise to God is completely appropriate, because in forming the Body before the world began, He chose us by His sovereign decree apart from any of our works. How we must praise Him for that! The doctrine of election allows God to be God.

How God can choose some, offer salvation to everyone, and then hold responsible those who weren't chosen is all a mystery to us. I don't know how God resolves those tensions, but I am content to leave the resolution with Him. The Bible clearly teaches both election and human responsibility. I have heard some believers say the truth lies somewhere in the middle. Not so! Both doctrines are fully true. Therefore, we need to let God be God and man be man and praise the Lord for His secrets. I get excited knowing that God loved me before I was born.

The Objects of Election

Please remember this, God didn't choose everyone to salvation. Jesus said, "And this is the will of Him who sent Me, that of all that He has given Me I lose nothing" (John 6:39). There is a Body that God has chosen to be a gift to Jesus Christ. Every believer is part of that love gift to Christ—a gift of the Father's love to His Son.

"For though the twins [Jacob and Esau] were not yet born, and had not done anything good or bad, in order that God's purpose according to His choice might stand, not because of works, but because of Him who calls, it was said to her [Rebekah], 'The older will serve the younger'" (Rom. 9:11-12). God actually determines salvation before the children are born. To those who claim that this is unjust, Paul answers, "What shall we say then? There is no injustice with God, is there? May it never be! For He says to Moses, 'I will have mercy on whom I have mercy, and I will have compassion on whom I have compassion'" (vv. 14-15), and "So then He has mercy on whom He desires, and He hardens whom He desires. You will say to me then, 'Why does He still find fault? For who resists His will?'" (vv. 18-19)

Why would God find fault in us if He didn't choose us? Paul's answer is, "On the contrary, who are you, O man, who answers back to God? [You have no right to question God.] The thing molded will not say to the molder, 'Why did you make me like this,' will it?" (v. 20)

Does the clay jump up and ask the potter why it looks the way it does? Not at all. Some believe that is terribly cold and calculating. But that is only one side of God's sovereign election. Paul writes, "If you confess with your mouth Jesus as Lord, and believe in your heart that God raised Him from the dead, you shall be saved; for with the heart man believes, resulting in righteousness, and with the mouth he confesses, resulting in salvation. For the Scripture says, 'Whoever believes in Him will not be disappointed' . . . for 'whoever will call upon the name of the Lord will be saved'" (10:9-11, 13).

How these two sides of God's truth—His sovereignty in choosing us (Rom. 9) and our responsibility to confess and believe (Rom. 10)—reconcile is impossible for us to understand. Scripture declares both perspectives of salvation to be true (John 1:12-13). It's our duty to acknowledge both and joyfully accept them by faith.

The Time of Election

Paul declares the time of God's election of the Body as occurring "before the foundation of the world" (Eph. 1:4). In eternity past God laid out all His plans: "The Lord . . . makes these things known from of old" (Acts 15:18). How much did He plan? Everything. "Then the King will say to those on His right, 'Come, you who are blessed of My Father, inherit the kingdom prepared for you from the foundation of the world'" (Matt. 25:34). He made the entire plan at once—the coming of Jesus Christ was part of it: "But with precious blood, as of a lamb unblemished and spotless, the blood of Christ. For He was foreknown before the foundation of the world" (1 Peter 1:19-20). Christ is called "the Lamb slain from the foundation of the world" (Rev. 13:8, KJV).

The Purpose of the Body

Why did God save some? "That we should be holy and blameless before Him" (Eph. 1:4).

God wants us to be "before Him"—in His own presence. He wants our fellowship. The entire Body of Christ is designed for fellowship with the Father (John 14:3; 17:24; 1 John 1:3).

However, we must meet some prerequisites if we are to have fellowship with God. Holiness is one. Anything unholy does not belong in God's presence. But the holiness of God's people was not automatic: "Christ also loved the church and gave Himself up for her; that He might sanctify her, having cleansed her by the washing of water with the word, that He might present to Himself the church in all her glory, having no spot or wrinkle or any such thing; but that she should be holy and blameless" (Eph. 5:25-27).

Paul also says Christians were chosen to be "blameless" (1:4). The Greek word *amomo* is used of a perfect lamb brought to the temple sacrifice. We must be blameless, or spotless, to have fellowship with God. Since only Jesus Christ is spotless, God had to impute to Christians Christ's spotlessness. Only in Christ can we go before God and enjoy His fellowship. Those who love Him are now in that fellowship.

The Motive for Election

Why did God do all this? Love motivated the formation of the Body—love generated election. Paul says, "In love He predestined us" (Eph. 1:4-5). Some people see predestination as a harsh doctrine, yet it came from the warmth of God's love. Every person who ever lived and will live deserves hell, yet love chose us. Look at your sin and worthlessness, then remember that even before you existed, God loved you and chose you. "In this is love, not that we loved God, but that He loved us" (1 John 4:10). It is exciting beyond words to know that God loves me and has loved me since eternity past. Now that's security! "Come, you who are blessed of My Father, inherit the kingdom prepared for you from the foundation of the world" (Matt. 25:34). "All that the Father gives Me shall come to Me . . . of all that He has given Me I lose nothing" (John 6:37, 39).

The Result of Election

When we love others, we naturally want them as close to us as possible. God loved us so much that He made us His children, adopting us into His family. Adoption is the result of election. "In love He predestined us in Jesus Christ for His sonship" (Eph. 1:5, MLB). That is as close as God could get us to Himself. Does that make us second-class children? No. Christ is not ashamed to call us His "brethren" (Heb. 2:11) and "fellow-heirs" (Rom. 8:17).

In Roman days, when a child was adopted, he or she received every right of a child born into a family. If the adopted one was in debt or in trouble for crime, the moment the child was adopted into a Roman family everything in his or her past was wiped clean. These children had no debts, owed nothing to society, their crimes were forgotten, and they started a new life. Everything their new father possessed was rightfully theirs.

Why did God want to redeem us?

> But when the fulness of the time came, God sent forth His Son, born of a woman, born under the Law, in order that He might redeem those who were under the Law, that we might receive the adoption as sons. And because you are sons, God has sent forth the Spirit of His Son into our hearts, crying, "Abba! Father!" Therefore you are no longer a slave, but a son; and if a son, then an heir through God (Gal. 4:4-7).

That ought to provide every believer with clear insight into his or her identity. When God says the believer is a son (or daughter), it means something. All the Father's love, all His spiritual blessings, belong to the Christian. The Father's care and the Father's gifts are ours. We have boldness to enter the Father's presence and to say "Father" in an intimate way. We have gained the promise of an inheritance. And we now have a place in the Father's house, with all the rights and privileges of sonship. All that is true of every Christian because God in eternity past chose us to be adopted into His family.

The Goal of the Body

In the ultimate sense, what does it mean to God to have us as sons? "According to the kind intention of His will, to the praise of the glory of His grace" (Eph. 1:5-6), and "the praise of His glory" (v. 12). That is the reason for everything God does. God's glory is the theme that runs throughout the Bible. "For it is God who is at work in you, both to will and to work for His good pleasure" (Phil. 2:13). Christians are a joy to the heart of God.

As a believer, you need to understand that you are not insignificant to God. You are specially loved by Him, chosen before the world began to receive His love and blessings, and to radiate Christ to unbelievers.

Paul warns, however, that every Christian should not "think more highly of himself than he ought to think" (Rom. 12:3). But some Christians may think too lowly. Something is wrong when a Christian doesn't bless the name of God every day for his or her place in the Body. How tragic that any Christian possessing these glorious privileges would dabble in sin and disobedience! You have no cause for a defeatist, inferior attitude. You are beloved by God and a part of the Body formed before the world began.

2

Know Your Position in the Body

When I played college football, my coaches constantly drilled our team with the admonition: "Play your position!" They had to repeat it often because when we saw the play develop toward another place on the field, we were tempted to dash over and try to tackle the guy with the ball. About that time the play would reverse direction to the spot we had just left.

One of our best players was very aggressive and often strayed far from his position. He was all over the field tackling people, and invariably the wrong ones. Finally, he was benched. Though he was a good athlete, he proved worthless to the team because he wouldn't stick to his position.

There's a parallel to this in Christian experience. God has put us on His team and given us both the resources and the obligation to "play" our positions in the Body of Christ. He gives us spiritual gifts for carrying out our assignments. In the football team's locker room, the coaches diagram plays on a chalkboard. Everyone's position is plain to see. The plays always develop perfectly on the chalkboard, because the figures representing the players always make the right moves. On the field it's a different story.

Christians must first find their positions in the Body of Christ. They must study the chalkboard, so to speak, and see where they stand, who's on either side of them, who's behind them, who's in front of them. They cannot be an effective participant in the Christian experience until they learn their place. Many Christians don't know how to live, partly because they don't know their positions.

In the first three chapters of Ephesians, the Apostle Paul presents the believer's position, the spiritual standing that God has given him or her in Christ. In the last three chapters Paul explains how "to play the game." Once Christians really know their position, their resources, and their power, they can get into the game wholeheartedly, with confidence that they can do the job. Otherwise, they will not function properly.

Basically, God's gift of salvation in Christ brings a believer into a position of righteousness. Man naturally is a sinner, separated from a holy God. But by virtue of our faith in Christ, we can know God. Christ's perfect righteousness is imputed to the believer. Though declared positionally righteous, believers still have sin in their lives. We are not righteous 100 percent of the time in our experiences, but we are exhorted, on the basis of our positional righteousness, to strive for righteousness in practice.

This theme runs throughout the New Testament: Christians are to become in practice what they are in position. In the Scriptures every believer is described as spiritually alive unto God, dead to sin, forgiven, declared righteous, a child of God, God's possession, an heir of God, blessed with all spiritual blessings, a citizen of heaven, a servant of God, free from the Law, crucified to the world, a light in the world, victorious over Satan, cleansed from sin, declared holy and blameless, set free in Christ from the power of sin, secure in Christ, knowing peace and rest, and led by the Holy Spirit.

You might be thinking, "The Bible may say all that, but I sure don't always live up to those descriptions." That is why in the New Testament, for every one of those statements of our position, there is a corresponding practice we're to follow. For example, since every Christian is spiritually alive to God, we're told to live that new life. Since we're dead to sin, we're not to give sin any place in our lives. Since we're forgiven, we're to count on it and not go through life feeling guilty. Since we've been declared righteous, we're to live righteously. Since we're children of God, we're told to act like God's children. Since we're God's possession, we're supposed to yield to Him. Since we're heirs of God, we're to add to our inheritance.

A Settled Position

I'm convinced that if believers would honestly study their positions, their lives would change. They would understand that failure in some aspect of Christian living doesn't mean they lose their position. In truth, a Christian's position is forever settled—it is unchanging, permanent. Sometimes believers think that when they have done something wrong, they have blown their salvation and are no longer righteous before God. That is false. Lack of growth and maturity never touch a Christian's position.

On the other hand, just as stumbling will not change a Christian's standing for the worse, neither will growth add to it for the better. Some people hold that the more mature you become in Christian experience, the more God likes you. As you grow, God becomes more gracious and loving. But God's favor does not depend on our works. God "has saved us, and called us with a holy calling, not according to our works, but according to His own purpose and grace which was granted us in Christ Jesus from all eternity" (2 Tim. 1:9).

God's grace existed before the world was created. We can't do one thing to earn His favor. From the moment of our salvation, we received the absolute favor of God—there is no degree to it. The Christian is "accepted in the beloved [Christ]" (Eph.1:6, KJV). We cannot increase or decrease in the favor of God. Nothing a Christian does, or fails to do, can change to the slightest degree his or her perfect standing before God.

When a normal baby is born, that baby has all his or her bodily parts. That baby doesn't begin life with one leg, for example, then grow another leg in two years and a nose eight months after. The growth process doesn't add new parts, but merely strengthens existing ones. That's how it is with Christians.

When we are created anew in Christ, we are created with all the necessary parts—nothing is missing. Christian growth strengthens what God has made us positionally. "I know that everything God does will remain forever; there is nothing to add to it and there is nothing to take from it" (Ecc. 3:14).

When God does a work, it's complete, and we are not able to add to it or take away from it. Instead of asking God for more parts, instead of seeking to be more favorable to God, we should be doing what the Apostle Paul prayed the Colossians would be doing: "Giving thanks to the Father, who has qualified us to share in the inheritance of the saints in light" (Col. 1:12).

The Christian is already fit. No attainment, no growth makes us any more favored or more complete—"in Him you have been made complete" (2:10). Paul is not speaking of the Christian's practice; he does not say the Christian is perfect in behavior. But because of salvation, the believer is complete in Christ. "For by one offering He [Christ] has perfected for all time those who are sanctified" (Heb. 10:14).

Yet that completeness does not mean that believers who understand their position will remain as they are—they will see changes in their lives. Throughout the New Testament, there is an emphasis on the believer's identity and his or her understanding and application of his or her positional resources. Mature Christians understand who they are and rely on their positional resources to handle the practical aspects of Christian living. Paul appeals to us to so live: "I, therefore, the prisoner of the Lord, entreat you to walk in a manner worthy of the calling with which you have been called" (Eph. 4:1).

A Prayer for Understanding

An interesting pattern recurs in Ephesians. In 1:1-14 Paul speaks of the believer's position, and in 1:15-23 he prays that we will understand our position. Again, in 2:1–3:12 he teaches us positional truth; then in 3:13-21 he prays that we will understand it. Twice Paul does it: position—prayer, position—prayer. Not until chapter 4 does he begin to explain how to practice the Christian life. The principle in Christian living, as in football, is this: You can't play your position until you know what it is. The Christian life is becoming in practice what we are in position.

Paul's prayer includes both thanksgiving and petition: "For this reason I too, having heard of the faith in the Lord Jesus which exists among you, and your love for all the saints, do not cease giving thanks for you, while making mention of you in my prayers" (1:15-16).

When Paul wrote the Epistle to the Ephesians, he was in prison in Rome. Four years had passed since he had been in Ephesus, but Christian travelers brought him word of events there, using the network of Roman roads and sea transportation. Paul felt a sincere bond of love with the Ephesian believers. They especially were concerned about his arrest, and they wanted to see him. Paul's heart was full of rejoicing, especially for two things he had learned about the Ephesians: their faith in Christ and their love for one another.

After assuring the Ephesians of his thankfulness for them, Paul's prayer becomes a petition to God that they might understand their position in Christ (v. 17). Unfortunately, many Christians are ignorant of their resources—and that is tragic! The Prophet Hosea noted this: "My people are destroyed for lack of knowledge" (Hosea 4:6). The Israelites were cut off from blessing because they didn't know God's Word. Many Christians stumble throughout their lives because they have no idea what their resources are.

What is more, God gives all believers equipment to understand their position and resources. The natural mind does not understand spiritual truth. If the brain were the key to spiritual understanding, the most intellectual persons would be the most Christlike. But note what Paul prays for: "that the God of our Lord Jesus Christ, the Father of glory, may give to you a spirit of wisdom and of revelation in the knowledge of Him" (Eph. 1:17).

The key to the verse is the word "spirit." It is not the Holy Spirit, because believers receive Him at the time of their conversions. "If anyone does not have the Spirit of Christ, he does not belong to Him" (Rom. 8:9). And Paul is not speaking of the so-called human spirit. How can we be given a human spirit when we already have one?

The Greek word for "spirit" (*pneuma*) means "wind, breath, and air," but it also refers to "an attitude, disposition, or influence." Paul was saying, in effect, "I'm praying that God will give you the attitude of wisdom and revelation" (Eph. 1:17). We use "spirit" that way in our day: Someone comes into the room looking gloomy, and you say, "You're in low spirits today." You mean his prevailing attitude is sad. Or, you may say, "Look at that gal! Boy, is she spirited!" You mean that her attitude is energetic, enthusiastic.

The loftiest thing Christians can do in this life is give themselves unstintingly and wholeheartedly to seek "wisdom and revelation." The Holy Spirit produces the right attitude in the believer and enables us to understand God's revelation.

> For to us God revealed them through the Spirit; for the Spirit searches all things, even the depths of God. For who among men knows the thoughts of a man except the spirit of the man, which is in him? Even so the thoughts of God no one knows except the Spirit of God. Now we have received, not the spirit of the world, but the Spirit who is from God, that we might know the things freely given to us by God (1 Cor. 2:10-12).

As the Holy Spirit works in us, He creates in us an attitude that hungers to know our resources. Every Christian needs such a disposition to hunger and thirst after the knowledge of God.

Christians know God through their faith in Christ, but Paul's concern is for a depth of knowledge that requires more than human intellect. The Holy Spirit alone can unearth the deep things of God and open the Christian's mind to "wisdom and revelation." Revelation refers to the facts, wisdom to the practical use of facts. The apostle considers both the content and the proper use of knowledge. There is a vast difference between "knowledge of spiritual things" and "spiritual knowledge." Many people may know a lot of theology, but lack wisdom to apply the facts. Some degree of divine illumination comes with salvation, but every Christian needs to plumb the deep things of God. Paul especially wants believers to know three things: the greatness of God's plan, the greatness of His power, and the greatness of His Son.

The Greatness of God's Plan
When we have the "spirit of wisdom and of revelation" (Eph. 1:17) in our hearts, our capacity for understanding the truth is enlarged, and we will have a greater grasp of God's plan than we had before. Paul describes this process as having "the eyes of your heart . . . enlightened, so that you may know what is the hope of His calling, what are the riches of the glory of His inheritance in the saints" (v. 18).

The word "heart" refers to the thinking process of the inner man.

The inner man must be enlightened to understand the hope of God's calling and the riches of His inheritance.

This enlightenment has nothing to do with IQ, but rather with sensitivity to the Holy Spirit. There are people who are not scholars who have keen spiritual insight. In contrast, some on the top of the academic ladder lack spiritual insight. The principle of spiritual enlightenment is in several New Testament verses: "'These are My words which I spoke to you while I was still with you, that all things which are written about Me in the Law of Moses and the Prophets and the Psalms must be fulfilled.' Then He opened their minds to understand the Scriptures" (Luke 24:44-45).

Those verses describe the process by which Jesus taught His disciples. Divine intervention alone can unlock our spiritual understanding. The natural man cannot do it—the truths about God's plan must be supernaturally revealed.

Lydia provides another example: "And a certain woman named Lydia, from the city of Thyatira, a seller of purple fabrics, a worshiper of God, was listening; and the Lord opened her heart to respond to the things spoken by Paul" (Acts 16:14).

The Lord opened her heart. Apart from the Holy Spirit's work in her heart, she could not understand the spiritual truths Paul was preaching. The Spirit is the illuminator.

Paul explains this principle: "The god of this world [the devil] has blinded the minds of the unbelieving, that they might not see the light of the gospel of the glory of Christ, who is the image of God. . . . For God, who said, 'Light shall shine out of darkness,' is the One who has shone in our hearts to give the light of the knowledge of the glory of God in the face of Christ" (2 Cor. 4:4, 6). Knowing the truth is the result of God making light shine within us.

Paul further stresses that believers should understand two aspects of God's plan: the hope of His calling and the riches of His inheritance (Eph. 1:18). The little phrase, "the hope of His calling," covers the length of time from eternity past to eternity future. "Calling" refers to God's election of the believer before the foundation of the world (see v. 4), while our "hope" is eternal life with Christ. Paul, in effect, prays that Christians will understand God's election in eternity past, His glory in eternity future, and all He has given the believer in between. The hope of our calling includes everything God has given the believer in our salvation. In another epistle the security of God's plan is revealed: "Faithful is He who calls you, and He also will bring it to pass" (1 Thes. 5:24). Our hope—our assurance—is that He will do what He says.

Based on that glorious truth, no believer should suffer from a spiritual inferiority complex. In the plan of God every believer is chosen, redeemed, declared righteous, made holy, and ultimately glorified. He said He would do it, and He did it. His Word assures our position in Christ and our resources. The secret of a proper Christian self-image is not to have an exalted view of oneself, but the right perspective of one's standing in Christ. To explore the depths of your position in Christ, you need to hunger for spiritual insight, which the Holy Spirit produces in your spirit as you search the Word of God.

The second aspect of God's great plan for enlightening believers is "the riches of the glory of His inheritance in the saints" (Eph. 1:18). "Saints," in the biblical sense, are those who have called on Christ in faith (1 Cor. 1:2). In God's master plan He has given believers an inheritance. All that God has is ours—endless riches for eternity.

It's impossible to describe precisely "the riches of the glory of His inheritance." Whatever it is, we know it is more than anyone will ever need. There is no bottom, no end to it. Indeed, Paul calls God's riches "unfathomable" (Eph. 3:8). But that doesn't keep him from talking about them—he mentions "the riches of His grace" (1:7); God's being "rich in mercy" (2:4); and "the riches of His glory" (3:16).

God's riches are sufficient for any situation a Christian may face. But how can you tap into them? By letting "the word of Christ richly dwell within you" (Col. 3:16).

When your mind is saturated with the Word of God, unending resources will flow. Fear, doubts, and anxiety will be destroyed. A mind filled with God's Word allows you to understand and appropriate your resources. As you plumb the depth of God's Word, you will realize that you are not just "in" God's plan, but that you *are* God's plan. Thus it is essential to have spiritual understanding of your position.

All my life I heard what I ought to do for God. I was told to be more dedicated, more committed, more consecrated; I was always being enjoined to do this and do that. I wondered if God had done anything for me—I just wanted someone to say, "Here's what God wants to do for you." That is the great blessing of knowing our position in Christ, knowing all that's ours because we are God's plan. That's why Paul prays for believers to understand the greatness of the plan.

The Greatness of God's Power

Here is the second resource Paul wants us to understand: "What is the surpassing greatness of His power toward us who believe. These are in accordance with the working of the strength of His might which He brought about in Christ, when He raised Him from the dead, and seated Him at His right hand in the heavenly places" (Eph. 1:19-20).

It's not enough to refer to God's power as great because it has "surpassing greatness." But what is that power?

"Power" in the Greek is *dunamis*, from which we get our word "dynamite." God's power in the believer is like a stick of dynamite. Christians ought to be exploding all over this world. Instead, many don't even fizzle; they may not even bother to light their fuses.

This power is not stagnant (or static); it is "working," which is the Greek word *energeia*, from which we get our word "energy." Christians are energized by almighty power, the same power that created the universe. But Paul describes it as the same power God used when He raised Christ from the dead and put Him at His right hand.

Many Christians wonder if they have ever experienced such power. They shouldn't wonder because that power is resident in them: "Having been buried with Him in baptism, in which you were also raised up with Him through faith in the working of God, who raised Him from the dead" (Col. 2:12). God showed His resurrection power at the point of our salvation; God made us alive in Christ. God's power was unleashed (cf. Acts 1:8). What a tragedy if that power lies dormant in us subsequent to our conversion. "And we proclaim Him, admonishing every man and teaching every man with all wisdom, that we may present every man complete in Christ. And for this purpose also I labor, striving according to His power, which mightily works within me" (Col. 1:28-29).

Paul shows how this power worked in his life as he labored to preach and teach Christ. Paul experienced God's power practically in his own life; thus he could speak of the gospel coming "in power" (1 Thes. 1:5).

God's power is still available for use now. Too many Christians, however, when asked to do something for Christ, wonder if they can handle it. But as we said earlier, there is no reason for any Christian to suffer from an emasculated spiritual image of himself or herself—not when he or she is supercharged with divine dynamite. Why chug along in your Christian life at five miles an hour when you have a unique power at your disposal. "Now to Him who is able to do exceeding abundantly beyond all that we ask or think, according to the power that works within us" (Eph. 3:20).

It would have been enough if Paul had said, "Christ is able to do what we ask," or, "He is able to do *beyond* all we can ask or think," or, "is able to do *abundantly beyond* all we can ask or think." But Paul goes on to define God's power at work in us as being "exceeding abundantly beyond all that we ask or think." It was this power Paul desired: "That I may know Him, and the power of His resurrection" (Phil. 3:10)—and the power he experienced: "I can do all things through Him who strengthens me" (4:13). May the same be true for every Christian!

The Greatness of God's Son

Paul then describes the third resource: "Far above all rule and authority and power and dominion, and every name that is named, not only in this age, but also in the one to come" (Eph. 1:21).

Christ is far above all ranks of angels, above Satan, above every power and authority in all history, or any yet to come. None is superior to Him. "And He put all things in subjection under His feet, and gave Him as head over all things to the church, which is His body, the fulness of Him who fills all in all" (vv. 22-23).

That is a symbolic reference to the king elevated above his subjects, who bow before him. It is the picture of the believer's position in Christ. Christians do not operate independently in this world; they are part of Christ's Body, the church, of which Christ is the Head. All life flows from Him; each member functions in Him. The

Head needs the Body to carry out its work; the Body needs the Head for direction.

When young Timothy was struggling with intimidation, persecution, and temptation, so much so that he had stomach trouble, Paul told him directly, "Remember Jesus Christ" (2 Tim. 2:8). Timothy was to take a little wine for his stomach trouble, and he was to "kindle afresh" his spiritual gifts, but Paul's supreme counsel was "Remember your resources in Christ."

Paul did not tell Timothy to rededicate or reconsecrate himself. Timothy simply needed to take a fresh look at Jesus. That Jesus was a descendant of David speaks of His humanity, while the phrase, "risen from the dead," proclaims His deity.

When Christians run into difficulty, they need to remember Christ's sympathetic understanding and divine power. There is no excuse for misunderstanding who Christ is.

In the Old Testament, when the Prophet Habakkuk was discouraged, he had to step back and consider God. Habakkuk faced a serious problem because Israel needed spiritual revival; and God's answer was to send judgment through the Chaldeans. Habakkuk was confused and angry. How could God use an ungodly nation to punish His people? Habakkuk thought he had God in a box, but God reaffirmed His plan, and Habakkuk had to back away from the problem and see himself from the right perspective. He told the Lord, in effect, that he didn't understand the problem or even how the Lord was dealing with it, but that he knew God was holy. Thus Habakkuk reaffirmed his trust in God. (See Hab. 1:12-13; 3:18-19.)

That is the way to solve every problem. You must forget the problem and remember who Jesus Christ is and what He came to do. Remember who is in you. There is no place for fearful, lukewarm believers. Do you really know your resources? Have you considered the greatness of God's plan and your place in it? Truly, every believer needs a spirit of wisdom and revelation in the knowledge of God's plan.

In Christ we are perfect positionally; but in practice we fall short. The Christian life is the experience of becoming in practice what we are in position. For every positional truth in the New Testament, there is a corresponding practice we are to follow. The following is a long but by no means exhaustive list.

POSITION	PRACTICE
2 Peter 1:3-4	2 Peter 1:5-8
Ephesians 1:3	Ephesians 4:1
Colossians 2:10	2 Timothy 3:17
Hebrews 10:14	Colossians 4:12
13:20-21	
Spiritually alive	*Live the life*
Ephesians 2:1, 4-5	Philippians 1:21
1 John 4:9	Galatians 2:20
John 11:25; 14:19	Romans 6:11-13
Acts 17:28	Titus 2:12
Dead to sin	*Don't give in to sin*
Ephesians 1:7	Romans 6:11-15
1 John 1:9; 2:12	Colossians 3:3
Romans 6:2-10	
Forgiven	*Count on it!*
Ephesians 1:7	Romans 8:1, 33-34
1 John 1:9; 2:12	
Colossians 1:14	
Made Righteous	*Live righteously*
Romans 1:17	2 Timothy 2:22
3:21-26	1 John 3:7
4:1, 3, 6	
5:17	
Children of God	*Act like God's children*
Ephesians 1:5	Ephesians 5:1
Galatians 3:26	1 Peter 1:13-14
God's possession	*Yield to God*
Ephesians 1:4	Romans 12:1
2 Timothy 2:19	2 Timothy 2:19-21

Heirs of God Romans 8:17 Colossians 1:12 Ephesians 1:11, 14, 18 1 Peter 1:3-4	*Add to your inheritance* Matthew 6:19-21 2 Corinthians 5:9-10 2 John 8 1 Corinthians 3:12-14
Blessed with all *spiritual blessings* *in the heavenlies* Ephesians 1:3 2:6-7 1 Peter 1:3-4	*Cherish those blessings* Colossians 3:1-2
Heavenly citizenship *(Not of this world)* Philippians 3:20 John 17:14-16 1 John 5:4-5	*Live as citizens of heaven* 1 John 2:15 Colossians 3:1-2 James 1:27
Servant of God 1 Corinthians 7:22-23 Romans 6:22	*Act like a servant* Romans 6:17-19 12:11 Hebrews 12:28
New life 2 Corinthians 5:17	*Walk in new life* Romans 6:4
Free from law Romans 6:14 7:1-6	*Yet keep fulfilling the Law* Galatians 5:1 Romans 8:4
Crucified to the world Galatians 1:4 6:14-15 Romans 12:2	*Avoid worldly things* 1 John 2:15-17 James 4:4

Light to the world 1 Thessalonians 5:5 Matthew 5:14	*Walk as children of light* Ephesians 5:8 Matthew 5:15-16
Victorious over Satan Revelation 12:9-11	*Claiming victory* Ephesians 6:11-17 James 4:7
Cleansed John 15:3 1 John 1:7, 9	*Cleanse yourself* 2 Corinthians 7:1 Philippians 4:8
Holy and without blame Ephesians 1:4 1 Corinthians 3:17	*Live holy lives* 1 John 3:7 1 Peter 1:15-16 2 Peter 3:14
Free John 8:32	*Enjoy your freedom* Galatians 5:1
In Christ Ephesians 1:3, 10 2:6, 13	*Abide in Him* 1 John 2:28
Secure in Christ 1 Peter 1:5 Romans 8 John 10:27-28	*Enjoy your security* 2 Peter 1:10
Possessors of peace Romans 5:1 14:17 John 14:27 Acts 10:36	*Let it rule* Romans 14:19 Colossians 3:15
One Ephesians 4:4-6	*Live that oneness* Ephesians 4:3

1:9-10	John 17:21
1 Corinthians 12:13	

In grace	*Grow in grace*
Romans 6:1	2 Peter 3:18

In fellowship	*Experience that fellowship*
1 John 1:3-7	1 Corinthians 10:20
	Ephesians 5:11

Joyful	*Experience that joy*
Romans 5:2	John 1:4
John 15:11	
16:24	
	Philippians 4:4

Spirit indwelt and led	*Yield to the Spirit's control*
1 Corinthians 6:19-20	Ephesians 5:18
Romans 8:9, 14	4:30
	1 Thessalonians 5:19
	Galatians 5:25

Spirit-gifted	*Use your gift*
1 Corinthians 12:4	Romans 12:3-6
Romans 12:5-6	1 Peter 4:11

Empowered for service	*Claim and demonstrate that power*
Acts 1:8	1 Corinthians 2:4
Ephesians 3:20	Philippians 3:10
2 Corinthians 4:7	Ephesians 6:10
2 Timothy 1:7	Philippians 4:13

Love	*Love!*
Romans 5:5	1 Peter 1:22
1 John 2:5	4:8
5:1	John 13:34-35
3:18	

3

Salvation: Entrance to the Body

Some years ago I had the opportunity to address a group of Hollywood film people, and I invited those desiring to receive Christ as their personal Savior to see me afterward. Soon a young, handsome Muslim from India approached me. When I told him how to trust in Jesus for salvation, he prayed and committed his life to Christ. Then he stood up, shook my hand, and said, "Isn't it wonderful! Now I have two gods—Jesus and Muhammad."

He thought he could choose several options. I explained his error. But his confusion was no worse than that of many Americans when it comes to understanding what a Christian really is. Some will say a person who lives in America, or who loves his or her mother, or who goes to church, or who believes in God and is basically a good, moral person is a Christian. Because of this confusion, it is vital to analyze how the Scriptures define a Christian. As clearly as anywhere in the Bible, we find such a description in Ephesians. We've seen that the epistle explains how all Christians can be certain of their positions in the Body of Christ, and that all believers can know their resources as members of that Body. At this point in his letter to the Ephesians, the Apostle Paul pauses to review how one enters the Body. There is only one way—Jesus Christ. Paul reveals six facts necessary to a clear understanding of salvation (Eph. 2:1-10). We see that we are saved from sin, by love, into life, with purpose, through faith, and for good works.

Salvation Is from Sin

While many people claim they believe in Jesus, they have not turned from sin. Yet there is no saved person who has not turned from sin. That does not mean we become sinless, but our life pattern has changed from a pursuit of sinfulness to a pursuit of godliness. It must be that way, for the Scripture says, "If any man is in Christ, he is a new creature; the old things passed away; behold, new things have come" (2 Cor. 5:17).

Paul first describes our sinful state and practice this way:

> And you were dead in your trespasses and sins, in which you for-merly walked according to the course of this world, according to the prince of the power of the air, of the spirit that is now working in the sons of disobedience. Among them we too all formerly lived in the lusts of our flesh, indulging the desires of the flesh and of the mind, and were by nature children of wrath, even as the rest (Eph. 2:1-3).

The natural man comes into the world spiritually dead and alienated from the life of God. Our basic problem is not disharmony with other people, but alienation from God.

Many years ago I was studying in my office when a mother who lived in the neighborhood surrounding Grace Community Church rushed in frantically asking for help. I followed her to her home to discover that her baby had died less than a half hour earlier. In fact, the body was still warm. No stronger stimulus exists in humanity than that between a mother and her baby, but no matter how hard she tried, that mother could not revive her baby. Death means complete inability to respond, whatever the stimulus. That is how we are born into this world—spiritually. We cannot react to the stimulus of divine truth because our inner man is dead. We cannot sense the impulses of the divine world nor feel the heartbeat of spiritual reality.

A natural man can sit in a church pew and wonder what other people get out of the service. He can read the Bible and not understand any of it. He can listen to Christians testify about how they live for the glory of God instead of for self and be mystified as to why believers would want to give up everything that's really fun in life.

One day as some men talked about following Jesus, one said, " 'Lord, permit me first to go and bury my father.' But Jesus said to him, 'Follow Me; and allow the dead to bury their own dead'" (Matt. 8:21-22).

Jesus' response brought to light the nature of physical and spiritual death. This potential disciple wanted to delay following Christ until after his father died, because then he could cash in on the inheritance. Yet his father was still living. Jesus replied, in effect, "Let the spiritually dead bury the physically dead." Unbelievers can take care of such things—what's important is giving oneself to the matters of the kingdom of God.

There are two kinds of death: death of the body, which we know as physical death, and death of the inner man, which is spiritual death. When we are born, we are spiritually dead.

Paul defines spiritual death as an active condition: "in . . . trespasses and sins." We are spiritually dead not "because of" sin but "in" sin. We are not sinners because we sin; we sin because we are born sinful. So, in addition to our inner spiritual deadness—our insensitivity to spiritual impulses from God—we are involved in sinning.

Two words describe our sinful condition. The Greek word for sin is *hamartia*, which literally means "to miss the mark," as when an arrow falls short of its target. The mark, of course, is God's perfect standard of righteousness (Matt. 5:48). Everyone fails to reach it. "For all have sinned and fall short of the glory of God" (Rom. 3:23).

Most people have an inaccurate concept of sin. They think of murder, robbery, rape, and drunkenness as sin, but they don't think of the average "good guy" as a sinner. Sin is not necessarily violent, but it is a failure to come up to the standard. A person may often reach the mark of human goodness, but since he or she cannot reach the mark of God's perfect holiness, he or she is still a sinner.

It's easy to confuse human goodness with the goodness only God can produce. Jesus said, "If you do good to those who do good to you, what credit is that to you? For even sinners do the same thing" (Luke 6:33). There's a sense in which sinners do good to one another, if others do good to them. That's human, civic good. When Luke was shipwrecked at Malta, he noted, "The natives showed us extraordinary kindness" (Acts 28:2). Many people are motivated by human goodness. You quite frequently see them donate their blood, food, and money for charitable purposes. But civic, humanitarian goodness cannot compare with God's spiritual goodness. The Scriptures say, "There is none righteous, not even one; there is none who understands, there is none who seeks for God; all have turned aside, together they have become useless; there is none who does good, there is not even one" (Rom. 3:10-12). The "good" referred to here is that produced by God. The best a natural man can do is human goodness.

The second word Paul uses to describe our spiritual condition is *paraptoma* ("trespasses"). Once referring to a slip or a fall, it eventually came to mean traveling on the wrong road—in this case, going another way than God's way. We not only fall short (*hamartia*), but we also go in the wrong direction (*paraptoma*). We try but miss and go our own way. "There is a way which seems right to a man, but its end is the way of death" (Prov. 14:12).

Unsaved people are dead in their trespasses and sins, and as such they can't feel godly impulses, and they don't understand divine truth. Often the only thing left for them is to follow the appeals of the world and the flesh and ultimately to fall victim to whatever tempts them the most. Though their spirit is insensitive, their body remains sensitive and they become the victims of bodily desires.

The first characteristic of this kind of life is that it is lived "according to the course of this world." Unsaved people do whatever is characteristic of people in the world. Whatever the world is promoting, they are buying. They indulge in the sins of the times. They are at home and in complete harmony with the spirit of the age. There is always a spirit, an attitude, an influence pervading the world, and unsaved people are captured by it.

The world system today promotes humanism. Humanism says humans are the ultimate end of everything: we are captains of our souls, masters of our fate. Yet we are impotent in our efforts to solve the tensions between parents and teenagers, between parents themselves, between workers and managers, and even between nations. Instead, we appear the victims of everything that's gone wrong: decaying cities, spiraling crime and divorce, air and water pollution, hunger and poverty, population explosion, and wars and threats of wars. Humankind is simply incapable of solving problems alone.

According to humanism, we are free to do whatever we want. The truth is, we have no such freedom. Why not? Paul says, "You formerly walked according to the course of this world, according to the prince of the power of the air" (Eph. 2:2). A person's life is controlled either by God or by Satan. When we rebel against God and disobey Him, we are not free; we remain a slave to the prince of demons himself.

The word for "prince" in Greek is *archon*, which means the first one in order, the highest in rank. Satan is the leader of a band of demons that inhabits the lower atmosphere. Scripture suggests there are three "heavens": the atmosphere around the earth, the stellar heavens, and the "heaven of heavens" where we'll abide with God. In the lower atmosphere encircling the earth, Satan controls and energizes a body of demons to corrupt humans: "For our struggle is not against flesh and blood, but against the rulers, against the powers, against the world-forces of this darkness, against the spiritual forces of wickedness in the heavenly places" (6:12). The battle is not only with people, but also with the prince of demons and his host of underlings.

Satan is active in the lives of unsaved people, energizing them to act on his behalf in his rebellion against God. Even an occasional good deed may be prompted by Satan to pacify people's conscience so they will think highly of themselves. But people are dupes in Satan's war against God. The devil is a "roaring lion" (1 Peter 5:8), devouring people and using them to fight against God's power and against godly principles in the world.

A second characteristic of the spiritually dead is that they are "sons of disobedience." Children, without being taught, know how to disobey parents. In this life, then, people constantly resist carrying out God's commands because what God tells them to do, Satan tells them not to do. For example, the Bible instructs a child, "Obey your parents," but Satan says, "Disobey." God tells husbands to love their wives, but Satan says, "Cheat on them; be unfaithful." The Bible tells wives to obey their husbands, but Satan tells them that's demeaning and old-fashioned. For everything God says, Satan shouts the opposite.

The third characteristic of the spiritually dead is that they live to fulfill physical desires selfishly. The Apostle Paul indicts Jews and Gentiles alike. He refers to the raw paganism and immorality of the Gentiles and the hypocritical self-righteousness of the Jews as "the desires of the flesh." The unsaved are filled with fleshly desires because their spirits do not receive godly impulses. Spiritually dead persons gain satisfaction from fulfilling such desires; for many, it is all they get out of their living death.

The Greek word translated "desires" (*adze*) can refer to the irrational or forbidden. It suggests desire beyond the point of reason, beyond comprehension. It is marked by strong will. Paul describes the outworking of *adze* as "immorality [adultery—sexual infidelity in marriage], impurity [other kinds of sexual immorality, even a dirty mind], sensuality [unrestrained abandonment to orgy], idolatry [worshiping false gods], sorcery [dabbling in the occult, such as witchcraft], enmities, strife, jealousy, outbursts of anger, disputes, dissensions, factions, envyings, drunkenness, carousings, and things like these" (Gal. 5:19-21). Notice that those characteristics are a catalog of what we see in our society today. That's because without God the inner man is spiritually dead.

The fourth trait of the unregenerate is that they are children of wrath. That means they are the object of God's judgment. Take a man who is dead in trespasses and sin, who follows the course of this world, who does what Satan wants, and fulfills the desires of the flesh, and you have a man who is right in the center of the target of God's judgment. "The wrath of God is revealed from heaven against all ungodliness and unrighteousness of men" (Rom. 1:18).

Salvation, then, is deliverance from sin—from both the state and practice of sinfulness.

Salvation Is by Love

People certainly are not lovable by virtue of their deeds and attitudes, yet love is necessary to reach down to us in our unregenerate condition. Our hopelessness can be remedied only if God intervenes. The picture of humankind is dismal indeed, but the ray of hope is God's great love: "But God, being rich in mercy, because of His great love with which He loved us" (Eph. 2:4). It is staggering to contemplate that in view of our condition, God would still love us. But His love does not depend on how good we are. It is His character to love.

God's love is shown in the richness of His mercy. We need nothing so much as mercy. If we got what we deserved, we would quickly be judged guilty, without hope. Instead it's as if God came into court and said, "You're guilty, but you may go free." If you asked Him why, He would say, "Because I love you." Yet God is also just, and He does not discard His justice in this case. That is the reason Jesus had to die for sinners. He met the terms of justice so the sinner could have mercy. Someone had to die, because the just penalty for sin is death. Once the justice of God was satisfied in Christ, God could extend His mercy to sinful men and women.

Perhaps we should think of mercy and grace as two sides of God's love. Mercy means not giving us what we deserve. Grace is giving us what we don't deserve. Mercy holds back judgment; grace gives pardon. In His mercy God says, "I'll hold back judgment." In His grace God says, "I'll give you salvation." Mercy withholds God's wrath; grace releases His forgiveness. Mercy pities us; grace pardons us. Only love can prompt mercy and grace.

We can measure God's love by the cross. If we were to ask God to define His love, He might say, "Do you see that rocky ridge outside Jerusalem? Do you see three crosses? My Son died on the one in the middle. That's how much I love you." Our sin is not so much a crime against God's law as against His love. There is a difference. Someone has illustrated it this way:

> Suppose while driving my car, I ran a red light and hit and killed a little boy. I would be charged with manslaughter. I would have to pay everything I owe to the state in terms of fines and imprisonment. Once I've fulfilled that obligation, the state has no further claim on me. But there remains another matter to be settled. I must make right my relationship with the mother. I committed a crime against love, not just against the law. While a sentence satisfies the law, only the wronged person's forgiveness can satisfy a crime against love. There's no price tag on that. For my crime against love, I'm at the mercy of the person I've wronged. I must wait until that mother freely forgives me.

We break God's Law and sin against His love throughout our lives. The only way we become right with Him is when God says, "I forgive you." Our salvation is the act of His forgiveness, because He loves us.

Salvation Is into Life

When Christ enters a person's life, He makes that spiritually dead person alive and sensitive to God. "Even when we were dead in our transgressions, [God] made us alive together with Christ" (Eph. 2:5). That's when the Word of God begins to speak to us. Christian love now has meaning, and so does fellowship with other believers. We start to look at the world in a different light.

We need spiritual life. In fact, Jesus says to us, "I'll give you that life, because I am that life" (see John 14:6). Being alive "together with Christ" means a believer is identified in Christ's death and resurrection. Paul said, "I have been crucified with Christ; and it is no longer I who live, but Christ lives in me" (Gal. 2:20). Christ's death became mine when I received Him and rose in newness of life. Because I identified myself with Him, my old life was put to death. Because of His resurrection, I live.

All Christians are totally identified with Christ. Our lives are not our own; Christ lives in us. We are no longer held in bondage by the desires of the flesh, instead we break free from the shackles of sin and bask in Christ's freedom. That's what being spiritually alive means.

Salvation Has a Purpose

God had a purpose in mind when He planned salvation: God "raised us up with Him, and seated us with Him in the heavenly places, in Christ Jesus, in order that in the ages to come He might show the surpassing riches of His grace in kindness toward us in Christ Jesus" (Eph. 2:6-7). The believer died with Christ, rose with Him, and now lives a new kind of life. We actually sit with Christ in the heavenlies; that is the new sphere of our spiritual existence—"for our citizenship is in heaven" (Phil. 3:20). The Christian is living eternal life right now; we live forever in a world where God is real and Christ exists.

Beyond that, the believer's future is secure because of what God has done for us in Christ. Notice how Paul uses the past tense in Ephesians 2:6. When the Greeks wanted to speak of things that were secure, they used the past tense. When they wanted to talk about something that couldn't change, that was inevitable, they expressed it as if it had already happened. The Christian's place in heaven is secure because God guaranteed it.

God's purpose is for Christians to be the great trophies of His grace, displayed before all the angels for eternity. God's glory, grace, love, and mercy are nowhere as great as in the lives of those He has redeemed. When we look at what we were before our conversions (Eph. 2:1-3), we understand why we are the greatest expression of His grace. We were at the bottom, but God gathered us up and placed us in heaven, so the angels might marvel and praise Him for what He did in His redemptive plan (3:10).

Everything exists for God's glory; thus He puts us on display. God receives the glory for what He has done in us. Someday, when we bodily go to heaven, we will show the host of heaven for eternity that God truly deserves glory:

> After these things I looked, and behold, a great multitude, which no one could count, from every nation and all tribes and peoples and tongues, standing before the throne and before the Lamb, clothed in white robes, and palm branches were in their hands; and they cry out with a loud voice, saying, "Salvation to our God who sits on the throne, and to the Lamb." And all the angels were standing around the throne . . . and they fell on their faces before the throne and worshiped God, saying, "Amen, blessing and glory and wisdom and thanksgiving and honor and power and might, be to our God forever and ever. Amen" (Rev. 7:9-12).

Why are angels praising God? Because of His redemptive work. The great multitude comprises the trophies of His grace, and they glorify God so much that the host of heaven breaks out into joyful praise. Considering where we came from and what we will be, we should never stop thanking God for His wisdom, mercy, and love.

Salvation Is through Faith

Saving faith is the gift of God: "For by grace you have been saved through faith; and that not of yourselves, it is the gift of God; not as a result of works, that no one should boast" (Eph. 2:8-9). God gave us His love, mercy, and grace, and then the faith to respond. Faith in itself is not a human work that earns salvation. Salvation is "not as a result of works," not even of faith as a work. God *gives* faith. If faith were of ourselves, we could say, "See, I had sense enough to put my faith in God." But, no, that would be boasting of works. Paul states that God gives us faith along with everything else (see Phil. 1:29). The spiritual realm opens to the dead natural man only when God in His sovereign grace opens his or her spiritual understanding. By faith, we respond, and that is spiritual rebirth. By the miracle of regeneration a dead person becomes alive to the spiritual dimension and enters the mainstream of the life of God.

This spiritual truth may be illustrated by human birth. When a baby is born, the doctor slaps the infant's bottom and it cries and begins to breathe on its own. Is the baby smart enough to know that if it's going to stay alive it has to breathe. No, the truth is, it breathes because it was whacked and felt pain. It instinctively cries. Why does a person breathe spiritually through faith? Because God, as it were, slaps us with divine grace. Faith is merely a response to the grace of God, which jolts someone into spiritual life.

Thus the Bible speaks of conversion as a new birth from above (John 3:3-8). New birth is a gift that cannot be earned. A baby can't bring itself into life. The same is true with spiritual life—God must bring it into existence. All we do is respond in faith and accept our new life.

Salvation Is for Good Works

Salvation is not a result of human works such as confirmation, baptism, church membership, church attendance, Communion, keeping the Ten Commandments, living by the Sermon on the Mount, giving to charity, or being a good neighbor. Doing one or all of those things will not bring us from spiritual death to life. However, once we are reborn by faith in Christ, our lives are to be characterized by good works. Believers are saved *for* good works, not *by* them.

A Christian is also God's "workmanship" (Eph. 2:10), a word which in Greek may mean "masterpiece." As God's masterpiece, the

Christian is to continue doing good works. God gives the believer new life in Christ; daily He is molding us into Christ's likeness.

A Sunday School teacher explaining Creation was irritated by one boy in the class. Thinking to shock the pupil, the teacher asked, "Who made you?"

"God did," the boy replied.

"Well, He didn't do a very good job!"

The boy retorted, "That's 'cause He ain't finished with me yet!"

In a practical sense, the boy was right.

The believer is to walk in the good works that God has "prepared beforehand" for us. The Christian is saved "for" good works; now we are to do them. That is part of our salvation—it produces good works now. God has equipped His people to carry out His plan, which begins with the gift of faith and continues in the lifelong process of entering into good works. The Apostle John tells us the end of this process: "Beloved, now we are children of God, and it has not appeared as yet what we shall be. We know that, when He [Christ] should appear, we shall be like Him, because we shall see Him just as He is" (1 John 3:2).

"We shall be like Him" because God saved us from sin and death, giving us the life of Christ. He acts in love, gives us faith to respond to that love, designs good works for us to walk in, and plans to display us before angels. Such is the scope of salvation.

4

Releasing Power
in the Body

Christian experience is a matter of applying God's power to the needs of everyday living. But many times Christians are frustrated because they don't know how to activate God's power. My car has a lot of power under the hood. But I must take the key, put it into the ignition switch, and turn it on, or none of that horsepower will do anything. If I know how every part of my car operates, and if every part is in perfect working order, I could say to my car, "Take me to the store," and it won't move. I have to use the key to turn on the power.

Paul prayed that Christians would learn how to ignite God's power:

> For this reason, I bow my knees before the Father, from whom every family in heaven and on earth derives its name, that He would grant you, according to the riches of His glory, to be strengthened with power through His Spirit in the inner man; so that Christ may dwell in your hearts through faith; and that you, being rooted and grounded in love, may be able to comprehend with all the saints what is the breadth and length and height and depth, and to know the love of Christ which surpasses knowledge, that you may be filled up to all the fulness of God. Now to Him who is able to do exceeding abundantly beyond all that we ask or think, according to the power that works within us, to Him be the glory in the church and in Christ Jesus to all generations forever and ever. Amen (Eph. 3:14-21).

This prayer outlines five aspects of the power available to those in the Body: inner strength, the indwelling Christ, incomprehensible love, infinite fullness, and immeasurable power. From this prayer we learn how to use God's power in our lives.

Inner Strength

The first key to using God's power is inner strength. To understand Paul's purpose for this prayer, we must connect it to Ephesians 3:1-14. That passage is a kind of parenthetical aside in Paul's thought: "For this reason I, Paul, the prisoner of Christ Jesus for the sake of you Gentiles. . . . For this reason, I bow my knees before the Father" (3:1, 14). Paul repeats himself to show he is resuming his train of thought. Then he reviews the truths of God's plan and goes on to worship God as well as to pray for the church.

Paul is driven to his knees by the sheer realization of all the resources he has in God's plan. He describes God as the Father "from whom every family in heaven and on earth derives its name" (v. 15). One body and one family is the emphasis in Ephesians. The church is God's family because all believers are His children. All believers "have . . . access in one Spirit to the Father" (2:18); all constitute "God's household" (v. 19).

Paul is about to make a request to God, but he prefaces his request by acknowledging God as his Father. When we go to God, we do not approach Him in the spirit of fear; instead we cry, "Abba, Father," because we know the Father loves us. We go to Him with boldness and confidence. Paul prays that God will grant his request "according to the riches of His glory" (3:16). He asks that all God's attributes, all the depth of His glory, be at the disposal of the Christian. If a rich man gives you something out of his riches, it may be 25 cents; but if he gives you something according to his riches, it will be to the outer limits of his wealth. That's the way God gives. Salvation is "according to the riches of His grace" (1:7). Paul believed God would supply all his needs "according to His riches in glory" (Phil. 4:19). You may face serious problems that are seemingly insoluble, but God's riches are infinitely available to you. In Christ they are "unfathomable" (Eph. 3:8).

On the basis of such wealth at his disposal, Paul prays for strength "in the inner man" (v. 16). As we yield our lives day by day to the Holy Spirit, we gain strength within.

All believers need inner strength today in view of the unique emotional and physical pressures that weigh us down, knock us off balance, and lead us to despair, discouragement, and hopelessness. A weak inner man won't stand under the pressure.

If the inner man is weak, sin takes over, and the believer can't resist. We may become frustrated, guilty, and out of balance emotionally, mentally, and spiritually. The mental strain may eventually lead to physical illness.

However, it is possible for the Christian's inner man to be "strengthened with power" (v. 16). Literally, this means "empowered with power." The supernatural power at the believer's disposal is so great that Paul uses two Greek words to describe it: *krataio* ("to make strong") and *dunamis* ("power"). Such is the dynamic power available to the inner man.

Since the Holy Spirit strengthens the inner man, we must understand the filling of the Spirit. Though all believers possess the Holy Spirit, some are weak spiritually. The filling of the Holy Spirit occurs only as we yield our lives completely to Him. That works out in the following way.

Life consists of a host of decisions. If a man is filled with the Holy Spirit, he says, in effect, "I have to make a decision. Show me the way to go." If he sees a temptation coming, he allows the Holy Spirit to meet it and defeat Satan. The Spirit-filled life is living in Spirit-awareness.

This relationship is not complicated. It simply means taking one step at a time, allowing the Holy Spirit to be in charge. This relationship is developed by the discipline of regular Bible study and prayer. God's Word reveals the mind of the Spirit and in prayer we daily commit ourselves to Him.

Being filled is similar to a hand and a glove. By itself a glove does nothing; but if I put my hand into it, the glove is under my control. The glove doesn't argue and resist—it moves under the control of my fingers. The glove's only strength is my hand. In a similar manner, the Christian's strength is the Holy Spirit.

Paul prayed for other believers to be strengthened internally, as God had strengthened him. "My grace is sufficient for you, for power is perfected in weakness" (2 Cor. 12:9). Paul accepted this principle of divine working and rejoiced in it. He responded to God, "Most gladly, therefore, I will rather boast about my weaknesses, that the power of Christ may dwell in me. Therefore I am well content with weaknesses, with insults, with distresses, with persecutions, with difficulties, for Christ's sake; for when I am weak, then I am strong" (vv. 9-10).

How did this work out practically for Paul? When he left Ephesus for the last time, the Holy Spirit revealed that "bonds and afflictions" awaited him (Acts 20:23). Nevertheless, he went ahead resolving that "I do not consider my life of any account as dear to myself, in order that I may finish my course, and the ministry which I received from the Lord Jesus, to testify solemnly of the gospel of the grace of God" (v. 24).

He faced affliction confidently in the strength of the Holy Spirit, and later recounted it:

> In far more labors, in far more imprisonments, beaten times without number, often in danger of death. Five times I received from the Jews thirty-nine lashes. Three times I was beaten with rods, once I was stoned, three times I was shipwrecked, a night and a day I have spent in the deep. I have been on frequent journeys, in dangers from rivers, dangers from robbers, dangers from my countrymen, dangers from the Gentiles, dangers in the city, dangers in the wilderness, dangers on the sea, dangers among false brethren; I have been in labor and hardship, through many sleepless nights, in hunger and thirst, often without food, in cold and exposure. Apart from such external things, there is the daily pressure upon me of concern for all the churches (2 Cor. 11:23-28).

What a catalog of experiences! Paul was not nervous and defeated. He was strong in the inner man, because he was filled by the Holy Spirit and allowed the Spirit to direct his life. Here is further testimony:

> We are afflicted in every way, but not crushed; perplexed, but not despairing; persecuted, but not forsaken; struck down, but not destroyed; always carrying about in the body the dying of Jesus, that

the life of Jesus also may be manifested in our body. . . . Therefore we do not lose heart, but though our outer man is decaying, yet our inner man is being renewed day by day (4:8-10, 16).

Only in the Holy Spirit did Paul have that kind of power. The first step to unleashing power in the Body is to lay hold of inner strength by the Holy Spirit. If the Christian is weak inside, nothing will happen.

The Indwelling Christ

As the Holy Spirit strengthens our inner man, Christ dwells in our hearts. Paul is not referring to Christ's indwelling believers in salvation, but in sanctification. The distinction appears in the Greek word used for "dwell," *katoikeō*, which means literally "to settle down." It carries the idea of coming into a home and settling down there. When a Christian is strong within, Christ, who is already there, settles down and feels at home. Believers must ask themselves whether Jesus is comfortable in their heart. When there is sin and disobedience, Christ is not at home.

In his booklet, *My Heart Christ's Home* (Downers Grove, Ill.: InterVarsity Press), Robert Munger gives a simple but vivid illustration of this spiritual principle. He compares his heart to a home. Since Christ has come there to live, He asks to go through it. First, He goes to the library—the control room, the brain, where all the thoughts and information are stored. Jesus finds evil and untruth. That has to go, so the man cleans it out. In the library there should be a portrait of Jesus, a reminder that Jesus is at the center of his consciousness.

Next is the dining room, the room of appetites and desires. Jesus asks the man what he longs for. He wants leeks, garlic, and onions—all the worldly delights. Jesus says, "If you want food that really satisfies, seek the will of My Father."

When they enter the living room, Jesus says, "You know, I sit in the living room every morning and you come right through here so fast you never stop to talk to Me." The living room represents fellowship, conversation, sharing. Jesus says, "I've been a guest in your house, but you don't talk to Me."

In the workshop Jesus sees many toys the man has made with his tools. "Is that what you've done with your skills?" He asks. "Use your talents and your abilities for the kingdom of God." Jesus should control this room too.

Finally, the man and his Savior return upstairs, only to encounter a strange odor coming from the hall closet. It represents secret sins. The man is upset; he figures if Jesus controls the dining room, living room, library, and workshop, that should be enough. But the odor persists. So Jesus asks him to open the closet door, and the things he didn't want to turn over to Jesus have to come out.

Only when Jesus controls every room is He really at home in our hearts. That can happen only through the indwelling Holy Spirit. The Spirit's work is to lovingly cause every believer to submit to His control and to gently lead each one to yield every part of his or her life to Jesus Christ. The result of being filled with the Spirit is strength in the inner man. As the inner man strengthens, Jesus cleanses the "heart home" and is at rest there. In wondrous condescension, He is willing to leave the infinite majesty of heaven and make His home in us. Jesus said, "If anyone loves Me, he will keep My word; and My Father will love him, and We will come to him, and make Our abode with him" (John 14:23). Jesus wants to "settle down" in the life of each believer.

Incomprehensible Love

When Christ settles down in a believer's life, love grows. Using the metaphor of planting a tree, Paul says that when Christ dwells in our hearts we are "rooted and grounded in love" (Eph. 3:17). Jesus said, "A new commandment I give to you, that you love one another, even as I have loved you, that you also love one another. By this all men will know that you are My disciples, if you have love for one another" (John 13:34-35).

When the world fails to recognize Christians, that means believers lack love for one another. God loves the world and wants to demonstrate that love through His people. That can happen only when Christians yield themselves to the Holy Spirit, are strong in the inner man, and allow Jesus to fill their lives. Then love will burst forth, because it is Jesus' nature to love. He will show His love if He has an open channel.

Peter echoes those thoughts: "Who through Him [Christ] are believers in God, who raised Him from the dead and gave Him glory, so that your faith and hope are in God. Since you have in obedience to the truth purified your souls for a sincere love of the brethren, fervently love one another from the heart" (1 Peter 1:21-22).

Before Christians can love people fervently, we must be established in love. Before we can be established in love, we must have a pure heart. To have a pure heart we must resist temptation. To resist temptation we must be strong in the inner man. To be strong in the inner man we must be controlled by the Holy Spirit.

When we are filled with the Spirit, we are not done with our responsibility. That is only the beginning. When Christ settles down in our lives, many things happen. Love is the by-product of this spiritual process: "That you . . . may be able to comprehend with all the saints what is the breadth and length and height and depth, and to know the love of Christ which surpasses knowledge" (Eph. 3:17-19).

The only way to comprehend the love of Christ is to be rooted and grounded in it. Someone asked Louis Armstrong about jazz, and the famous trumpeter said, "Man, if I got to explain it, you ain't got it." That's how it is with love. If a person has to tell you what it is, you don't have it.

If you are a parent, and someone tells you, "I really love my little child," you understand. But children don't always understand how much a parent can love, because they aren't parents.

"Comprehend" in the Greek is *katalambano*, which means "to seize" something and make it one's own. The only way we can seize the love of Christ and comprehend it, is to be grounded in it.

Christ's love is so great it is expressed in four dimensions: breadth, length, depth, and height. First-century Christians used the cross as the symbol of Christ's love. The post points upward and downward (height and depth); the crosspiece points to the horizons (breadth and length).

The letter to the Ephesians itself reveals the extent of Christ's love. The *breadth* of Christ's love reaches to the Jew on the one hand and the Gentile on the other (2:16-18). Its *length* is eternity past to eternity future. He chose believers "before the foundation of the world . . . in love" (1:4).

Christ's love is so deep it reaches down into the pit of sin and spiritual death and pulls us out of it (2:1). The believer is then raised to sit with Jesus in heaven. We have been lifted from the pit to an exalted position in glory (v. 6).

A Christian should understand the dimensions of Christ's love when faced with what looks like a disastrous situation. Those who do so are able to say to God, "I can't wait to see how You will show me Your love in this." Every circumstance is an opportunity for the believer to reveal Christ's love.

Infinite Fullness

The next key is being "filled up to all the fulness of God" (Eph. 3:19). Having the fullness of God means total spiritual richness. It doesn't mean that all there is of God comes to dwell in the believer—that can't be. God does not move into you and limit Himself to your capacity. A good illustration of that is drawing a thimbleful of water from a lake. The thimble is filled with the lake, yet the whole lake is not in the thimble. The thimble doesn't diminish the lake, yet it has the "fullness" of the lake in the sense that it contains a particle of every ingredient of the water. All the essential character of that lake is in the thimble.

In the same way, when we have the fullness of God, we possess the essential characteristics of God. But God is not diminished. We can communicate what God is like to the world by radiating God out of the fullness we have.

Since God is love, a believer filled with the fullness of God will express godly love. Since God is wise, a believer filled with the fullness of God will express godly wisdom. Since God is holy, the believer filled with the fullness of God will display holiness. Since God is gracious, a believer filled with the fullness of God will communicate godly graciousness.

God deposits those attributes in the Christian in reduced measure, so the believer can love with divine love, judge with divine wisdom, and live with divine holiness—without being divine himself or herself. In a word, to be filled with all the fullness of God is to be Godlike: wise, just, holy, pure, loving, gracious, merciful. We meet too few Christians who have this fullness. But when we do, we recognize it. That's because a person who radiates the fullness of God is attractive and powerful.

Just contemplating such a truth is staggering. How could God take a worthless human being, a rebel against His love, and give this person His fullness? Our response ought to be "Thank You, God, for putting Your fullness in me. Thank You for helping me to radiate Your wonderful Person."

If the world is to understand that God is love, love must be seen in Christians. If people are to recognize that God is wise, they must see God's wisdom in believers. Christians are responsible to communicate who God is by their lives.

Immeasurable Power

Lest we think that in having the fullness of God we are at the summit, Paul turns to how we unleash God's power in our lives. Possessing God's power means that in the believer God can do things "abundantly beyond" what the person asks or thinks. God "is able to do . . . according to the power . . . within us" (Eph. 3:20-21).

Paul explains what he means: "But we have this treasure in earthen vessels, that the surpassing greatness of the power may be of God and not from ourselves" (2 Cor. 4:7). Each of us can see this power at work when we are aware of our own incapacities.

What is the answer for Christians who feel that their lives are worthless? Consider again the progressive development of power in the Body of Christ. It starts with the inner man made strong by the Holy Spirit. Christ makes Himself at home in us, and as a result we comprehend love. Then we are filled with the fullness of God and power is released in our lives.

The goal of this spiritual development is the glory of God. Some Christians ask, "Why bother with all this? I'm going to heaven anyway." We bother with it because God wants to be glorified in the church now (Eph. 3:21). Every believer should be able to say "Amen" to Paul's prayer, and in that way say, "Let it be so in my life."

Part 2
The Church:
Working in the World

5

Acting Like a Member in the Body

When people join an organization, they subscribe to its goals and agree to live by its rules and standards.

Membership in the Body of Christ also demands certain conduct. When we join God's family, we belong to the Heavenly Father and receive rights, privileges, and honors (Eph. 1–3). Our obedience shows that we share the goals of the Body and want to conform to what God requires. This is a conformity of love. If Christians fail to conform to the pattern of the Body, it's not because they lack guidelines; rather they lack love, for love fulfills the Law (see Rom. 13:10).

When we know the truth, our obvious duty is to prove that we know the truth. In Ephesians, Paul turns to writing about behavior with a "therefore" (4:1) as the link between the chapters on doctrine (1–3) and duty (4–6). Paul also makes this connection in Romans (12:1) after eleven chapters on doctrine, and in Galatians (5:1) after four chapters on doctrine.

The Body needs consistent doctrinal teaching. Teaching duty without doctrine deprives the believer of "all the counsel of God" (Acts 20:27, KJV). Separating duty from doctrine leads to a legalistic spirit or causes the believer to rely on subjective, emotional pep talks. Without doctrine, the believer lacks the true motive for Christian living. We need the solid facts of the Word of God rather than human appeals to duty.

The New Testament contains numerous references to the need

for knowing sound doctrine. We read that the Christian is "being renewed to a true knowledge" (Col. 3:10), that we are to "grow in the grace and knowledge of our Lord and Savior Jesus Christ" (2 Peter 3:18), and that knowledge is the key to good works (Col. 1:10). The basis of a solid spiritual foundation is knowledge.

Conduct Is Related to Knowledge

Paul was careful to delineate basic doctrine in his epistles because he knew a Christian's conduct is directly related to his or her knowledge of doctrine. "If then you have been raised up with Christ, keep seeking the things above. . . . Set your mind on the things above, not on the things that are on earth" (Col. 3:1-2). "As those who have been chosen of God, holy and beloved, put on a heart of compassion, kindness, humility, gentleness and patience" (v. 12).

The believer's position is "raised up with Christ." Based on that fact, we are supposed to behave in a certain manner. Duty follows position. Except for God Himself, no one is in a more exalted position than the Christian. But we have nothing to do with attaining our position; it is all of God. Therefore, the true Christian's response to his or her high position must be a humble, lowly walk.

The Call to the Worthy Walk

Paul himself was one who walked worthy of his calling—no matter what the price. He was faithful to his trust; he fulfilled his calling. Even though his obedient life led to a Roman prison, Paul remained loyal to his Lord.

Paul was also passionately concerned for the spiritual welfare of those whom he had been called to serve. The depth of his concern is revealed in the words: "I . . . entreat you" (Eph. 4:1). Our vocation in this verse is not our job, our profession, or our career, but rather our calling to salvation, to the Body of Christ. Paul's appeal for a worthy walk is rooted in his status as a prisoner in Rome, which is where he was when he wrote the Ephesian letter. However, he never considered himself a prisoner of Rome, but rather a prisoner of the Lord. His bondage was in the plan of God. Paul was confident that God, not the Roman government, was in control of his life. Previously he had been imprisoned in Philippi, and God saw fit to deliver him. If God had wanted him set free from the Romans, He could have delivered him.

How is Paul's appeal to the worthy walk related to his imprisonment? He believed we should be loyal to our calling in Christ no matter what the circumstances. Paul was saying, in effect, "Look, friends, I'm a prisoner. That's about as bad off as one can get, and I can still say, 'Walk worthy of your calling.' It may lead to jail, but don't consider that the important thing."

Paul cared so much because his purpose and passion in life was to "present every man complete in Christ" (Col. 1:28). The apostle simply begged people to live out their Christian commitments. He could not settle for less than total spiritual maturity in every believer to whom he ministered.

Paul's burden should be the burden of every pastor. If pastors don't yearn for the spiritual growth of their people and exhort them toward spiritual maturity, they should leave the ministry. Epaphras was one who labored fervently that believers would "stand perfect and fully assured in all the will of God" (4:12).

The word "walk" (Eph. 4:1) describes the Christian's daily conduct—his or her lifestyle. This idea is seen repeatedly in the New Testament: "That you may walk in a manner worthy of the God who calls you into His own kingdom and glory" (1 Thes. 2:12); "only conduct yourselves in a manner worthy of the gospel of Christ" (Phil. 1:27); "that you may walk in a manner worthy of the Lord, to please Him in all respects, bearing fruit in every good work and increasing in the knowledge of God" (Col. 1:10).

Perhaps the best explanation of the need to walk worthy is found in a phrase Paul uses in his letter to Titus: "that they may adorn the doctrine of God our Savior in every respect" (2:10). Because the Christian's calling is "upward" (Phil. 3:14), "holy" (2 Tim. 1:9), and "heavenly" (Heb. 3:1), we are supposed to live by a certain standard of conduct. A godly life reveals to unbelievers the various facets of God's transforming grace and love. A life of obedience to God, of holiness, humility, love, joy, and peace shines like so many precious jewels, adorning the truth.

Suppose, for example, you try to explain to an unbeliever the truth about God. This man has doubts. Then one day he encounters another believer who simply lives out God's truth before him. Christianity then becomes attractive and appealing to the unbeliever. That's how Christians, by their worthy walk, can adorn the doctrine of God in the eyes of the world. This is a great responsibility, but we can fulfill it. The early church multiplied as it obediently lived out its faith (Acts 9:31). If all believers today adorned the doctrine of God by godliness in their behavior, they would have a tremendous influence on the world.

Characteristics of the Worthy Walk

Having stressed the necessity of a worthy walk, Paul gives five characteristics of it: humility, gentleness, patience, forbearance, and unity (Eph. 4:2-3).

Humility

Humility is genuine submissiveness that comes from an association with Jesus Christ. A Christian can know a lot of doctrine, memorize Bible verses, be faithful to the church, and be involved in many Christian activities, but not be walking in humility.

Christians introduced the concept of humility to the first-century Greek world. Prior to that time, humility was not considered a virtue. In fact, the early Christians had to coin the word *tapeinophrosune*, translated "humility," because it did not appear in classical Greek.

When Christians look for an example of humility, they need look only at Christ. "Have this attitude in yourselves which was also in Christ Jesus" (Phil. 2:5). Real discipleship begins here.

Paul himself exemplified the characteristic of humility: "Serving the Lord with all humility and with tears and with trials which came upon me through the plots of the Jews" (Acts 20:19). This was part of his farewell statement to the elders at Ephesus. Thus, when he wrote to them later, they and the rest of the Ephesian church could recall the example of his life. Paul faced much opposition, but he persevered with humility.

Humility is hard to come by because it begins only when we honestly face ourselves. Bernard said, "Humility is the virtue by which a man becomes conscious of his own unworthiness." However, many people stroll through life behind a facade of pride because they don't have the courage to look at themselves and see who they really are—sinners who need Jesus Christ.

If we realize our need for Christ, it will help us live by the divine standard. People may think they rate high, but that's often when they measure themselves against mediocre standards. For example, when I was in high school football, I received a gold trophy as "player of the year." But when I got to college, I found there were a lot of other top players. When I went to a pro football training camp, I saw that I was really nothing special by professional standards. In track I was good enough to win ribbons at my school, but when I got into the finals of the county invitational meet, I didn't win one medal. At that level of competition, the standards were much higher.

A Christian may look outstanding compared to the alcoholic who lives down the street. But godless neighbors are not the believer's standard; our standard is Jesus Christ. No matter how good we think we are, we fall far short of Jesus' perfect standard. Such realization moves us toward humility.

God-awareness is another factor in humility. It is vital to realize that if it weren't for God, we wouldn't exist. Humility is acknowledging that God controls everything. When a person becomes too proud, God often reaffirms His sovereign control in that life and humbles the person.

Gentleness
The worthy walk starts with humility and continues with gentleness. Gentleness (translated "meekness" in the *King James* Bible) is the attitude of a person who submits to God's dealings without regret and to human wickedness without revenge. The gentle person doesn't continually insist on his or her rights; the gentle person would rather accept injustice for himself or herself than inflict it on someone else.

This does not mean the gentle person is insipid or spineless. These people have true character and backbone. It takes more strength to be gentle than to fight for rights. As Aristotle said, one who is gentle is angry only at the right time. If the gentle person is angry, it's because God is maligned, not because he or she is hurt. Gentle people are concerned about the sufferings of others, but they don't get upset when they themselves suffer.

Just as Jesus exemplified humility, so the Lord also modeled gentleness (see 2 Cor. 10:1). When people rejected Him, He didn't become bitter; He "endured the cross, despising the shame" (Heb. 12:2). Despite the wicked treatment He suffered at the hands of men, Jesus prayed, "Father forgive them; for they do not know what they are doing" (Luke 23:34).

Gentleness is really a spirit of submission. If it seems to be a downward step, remember how far down it was for Jesus. The One who made the world and sustains it became the gentle and lowly One, and set the pattern for a worthy Christian walk.

Think what beauty and power would characterize the Body of Christ if meekness and lowliness were the order of the day, with no one insisting on his or her own rights.

Patience

The third component of a worthy walk is patience. No matter how bad life gets, the patient person perseveres. Specifically, the word in the Greek, *makrothumia*, means taking whatever people dish out, bearing insult, injury, and complaint with patient endurance, without bitterness and irritation. The patient Christian loves and waits.

The Body of Christ needs patience. The Body often is fractured when believers make a big issue out of being offended. Instead, they should endure the offense, remember the worthy walk, and press on as Jesus did. The Christian is not called to retaliate, no matter how wronged he or she might feel (see 1 Cor. 6:7).

Forbearance

Paul describes the fourth characteristic of the worthy walk as "showing forbearance to one another in love" (Eph. 4:2). Forbearance is the outworking of the first three traits of the worthy walk. It means loving another Christian even though that person might offend. The forebearing believer has room in his or her love to accommodate others' mistakes.

The attitude of forbearance will say, "I know you didn't mean it. You shouldn't have acted like that, but I love you." That kind of spirit instantly heals breaches in the Body's fellowship. Whenever there is a problem in the Body, apply the salve of forbearance.

Jesus was forbearing in the face of slander, insult, and physical abuse. He expects the offended Christian to assume the same spirit He showed toward His persecutors. Peter describes and commands this attitude when he wrote, "Keep fervent in your love for one another, because love covers a multitude of sins" (1 Peter 4:8). If we love only perfection, then we don't have Christian love.

Unity

When the first four characteristics of the worthy walk are in operation, the fifth one, *unity*, will follow: "Being diligent to preserve the unity of the Spirit in the bond of peace" (Eph. 4:3). The key to obtaining unity is "being diligent to preserve" it. "Diligent" means putting forth an effort. When conflicts arise, decisions must be made to alleviate the problem. One decision would lead to discord; the other would preserve unity in the Body. The second decision is the one God wants us to make.

Notice that Ephesians 4:3 does not command Christians to *create* unity. We are already one Body in Christ. We must therefore keep the unity we already have. We don't need church conferences on unity, but we do need to encourage one another to live the kind of life that is humble, gentle, patient, and forbearing in love.

Acquiring those virtues depends on death to self. So long as self is at the center of life, so long as personal feelings and prestige have top priority, the worthy walk is unreachable. If self is first, the doctrine of God is not adorned, the believer is not really at peace with other believers, and the Body will not experience oneness.

Reasons for the Worthy Walk

In Ephesians 4:4-6, unity emerges as the reason for the worthy walk. Seven "unities" make up the basis for the walk.

One Body

First, God commands Christians to keep unity because there is "one body" (Eph. 4:4). There are many local assemblies and congregations, but one Body. Though Christians differ in race, custom, culture, national origin, and language, and may be educated, uneducated, rich, or poor, they are one in Christ. Some Christians are in heaven, some on earth, but all believers constitute Christ's Body.

The unity of the Body is intended to be a witness to the world. Jesus prayed for believers to express their oneness "that the world may believe that Thou didst send Me" (John 17:21). This oneness is a sign that the Father loved the world and sent His Son into it (v. 23).

If the church does not show true oneness, it appears to the world to be just another social organization with the same quarrels and divisions other groups have. (This is the kind of appearance sometimes given by denominational distinctives, which tend to fragment the Body rather than unify it.)

One Spirit

Along with the emphasis on one Body is the clear teaching of "one Spirit" (Eph. 4:4). The Holy Spirit is the source of Christian unity because He is the agent of the new birth (John 3:5-8), and consequently He lives within each individual believer (14:16-17; Rom. 8:9; 1 Cor. 12:13) and within the church collectively (cf. Eph. 2:22).

Because He indwells the Body, we can test whether or not a work is of the Spirit. If division arises within the Body, we can be sure the work is not of the Spirit. Such a test is very helpful in this day when so many religious expressions claim to be genuine.

The Holy Spirit was the sign of spiritual validity in the Book of Acts. The question of whether the Gentiles had really been saved without keeping the Jewish law was debated at the Jerusalem Council (Acts 15). Speaking of the converted Gentiles, Peter said, "God, who knows the heart, bore witness to them, giving them the Holy Spirit, just as He also did to us" (v. 8). At Pentecost the Holy Spirit came on the believing Jews at Jerusalem, and later, when the gospel went to the Gentiles, the Spirit came on them in the same way (8:17).

The Jewish believers needed reassurance that the Gentiles had received the same Spirit. One part of the Body must not say to another part, "We have something you don't have." The Holy Spirit is the common denominator to provide unity within the Body.

One Hope

Believers also share "one hope" (Eph. 4:4), even though the circumstances of our calling to that hope are different. The believer's hope is not wishful thinking; it is certainty. That's because the Holy Spirit has been given to each believer as a down payment: "the Spirit as a pledge" (2 Cor. 5:5). That word "pledge" means "first installment," something like an engagement ring. The Holy Spirit guarantees that believers will someday receive their inheritance, that their hope is sure.

One Lord

Every genuine Christian confesses and serves the same Lord Jesus Christ (Eph. 4:5). He is "one Lord" over all the members of His Body, who have a common commitment and allegiance.

In the Body, only Christ gives the orders. If Christians are in conflict, it is because they have not yet understood the Lord's will, or perhaps because they have not received their orders from Him at all. Such believers may be mistaking their own desires for the will of Christ. Each part of the Body needs to be in daily touch with Jesus Christ the head so directions are not confused.

Fidelity to one Lord is a recurring theme in the New Testament. Speaking to the Gentiles in the home of Cornelius, Peter declared, "God is not one to show partiality. . . . The word which He sent to the children of Israel, preaching peace through Jesus Christ" (Acts 10:34, 36). In that parenthetical remark, Peter assured the Gentiles that Jesus is their Lord too.

Romans 10:12 further asserts, "There is no distinction between Jew and Greek; for the same Lord is Lord of all, abounding in riches for all who call upon Him."

And Paul said to the Corinthians, "Yet for us there is but one God, the Father, from whom are all things, and we exist for Him; and one Lord, Jesus Christ" (1 Cor. 8:6).

One Faith

Ephesians 4:5 next refers to "one faith." First, this may refer to the believer's exercise of saving faith. Second, the expression may indicate the content of the gospel itself, the basic body of Christian truth.

In the first instance, the point is that the believer comes to one Lord by faith. No one comes to Him any other way. In Paul's day Jew and Gentile asked, "Are there two faith experiences or one?" The apostle answered, "If indeed God is one—and He will justify the circumcised [the Jews] by faith and the uncircumcised [the Gentiles] through faith" (Rom. 3:30). In other words, all Christians are saved by faith.

However, in addition to referring to the believer's salvation response, the word *faith* is also used in Scripture to mean a body of truth. Jude appeals to believers to "contend earnestly for the faith" (Jude 3). He tells them to build themselves up "on your [their] most holy faith" (v. 20). Paul refers to being "established in your faith" (Col. 2:7).

In Ephesians 4:5 the word refers to the doctrines God has revealed to us. In this sense there is only one faith, one body of truth. Too often members of the Body argue over differing interpretations of Scripture. But there is not a Calvinistic New Testament and an Arminian New Testament, not a Baptist New Testament and a Presbyterian New Testament. The Body of Christ was founded on one body of truth, one faith.

Each believer is responsible to study faithfully and diligently the basic doctrinal tenets. "Be diligent to present yourself approved to God as a workman who does not need to be ashamed, handling accurately the word of truth," Paul counseled Timothy (2 Tim. 2:15). Not only is a member of Christ's Body to know what the faith teaches, but also we are to hold that faith in love. We must forbear when a fellow member of the Body does not see a teaching in the same light. The Body needs prayerful interaction so that each member may be a corrective to the other. Our goal should be to express "one faith" simply, clearly, and accurately.

One Baptism

Next in the progression of "ones" is "one baptism" (Eph. 4:5). Bible scholars differ on whether this is the baptism of the Holy Spirit or the ordinance of water baptism. Since the concept of Spirit baptism is included in the truth of one Body and one Spirit (v. 4; cf. 1 Cor. 12:13), I believe this "baptism" refers to the ordinance.

The Body comprises those who have placed their faith in one Lord, and what follows this expression of faith, according to New Testament practice, is the ordinance of baptism. The rite of baptism itself does not save the person, but it is a sign and a public testimony that we have committed ourselves to Christ.

Baptism is a matter of obedience to the Lord. Jesus included it in His commission to the disciples (Matt. 28:19). The early Christians followed this command. Wherever there was a confession of faith in Christ, there was a public baptism.

Paul's point of "one baptism" obviously was meant to stress the oneness of Jew and Gentile. When people came to Christ, there was one baptism, not different baptisms according to one's ethnic background. The Jews, of course, had practiced distinctive ceremonial washings, and they baptized proselytes (converts to Judaism). But in the new economy of the gospel, there was to be only one baptism.

It is essential for us to obey Christ in baptism, just as we obey Him in other commands. The ordinance signifies our own identification with the death, burial, and resurrection of Jesus. Water baptism symbolizes the end of the old life and the beginning of the new life within the Body.

One God and Father

The work of the Trinity is revealed in Ephesians 4:4-6—the Holy Spirit (v. 4), God the Son (v. 5), and God the Father (v. 6). Verse 6 is the climax of this magnificent progression of thought, showing the total unity that is the reason for the believer's worthy walk. "One God and Father" is "over all and through all and in all." He sustains and guides the entire universe. What a source of assurance this is to the believer—God is in control of everything!

God expresses His loving and wise control in the believer. The God of the universe is the God of the individual. He is "in all," that is, in everyone who has trusted in Christ, every member of the Body. The Bible says not even a sparrow falls without His notice (Matt. 10:29). He cares about the seemingly insignificant: "Do you not know that you are a temple of God?" (1 Cor. 3:16) We are God-created, God-loved, God-controlled, God-sustained, and God-filled. Believers enjoy the peace and the power that result from having the very life of God in them.

God has done everything according to the sevenfold oneness of Ephesians 4:4-6. He wants the Body to display that oneness, even as the Trinity displays it. Unity is the essence of both our lofty position and our lowly walk.

6

Building Up the Body

The most heartbreaking thing in my ministry is not that some people don't respond to the gospel or that more people don't go to the mission field. The one thing that saddens me most is that some members of the Body remain spiritual babies all their lives.

God's plan to bring believers to maturity involves the work of the Holy Spirit through human instruments. "He gave some as apostles, and some as prophets, and some as evangelists, and some as pastors and teachers" (Eph. 4:11).

Why did God give these? "For the equipping of the saints." "Saints" are believers, all members of the Body. God gave the early church apostles and prophets to equip the saints. He also gave evangelists and teaching-pastors to equip the saints.

Apostles, prophets, evangelists, and pastor-teachers are gifted believers given to the Body of Christ so that Christians might be brought to maturity. They are the agents of change in the life of the church; they are channels for the flow of dynamic energy for spiritual growth; they are catalysts for experiential maturity. The result of their ministry is the Body built up in love (v. 16).

Progress to Maturity

According to Ephesians 4, Paul outlines specific steps in the Body's maturing process. First, as already noted, gifted believers equip the saints (vv. 11-12). The Lord Jesus Christ won them at the cross and gave them to the church so that His children might be perfectly equipped and mature in their faith. Spiritual gifts for believers *en masse* are not in view here, but the specific gifts for those whom God has appointed as leaders of the Body. Their ministries are listed chronologically according to God's plan for the development of the church.

The apostles were a small group, originally appointed by Jesus Himself. They stood in unique relation to the incarnate Lord. They were His constant companions, witnesses to what He had said and done, "sent ones" to preach, heal, and cast out demons. After the defection of Judas, Matthias was chosen to fill the ranks. To the Twelve Jesus gave the Great Commission. The apostles became the authoritative source of truth about Christ, as John explained: "What was from the beginning, what we have heard, what we have seen with our eyes, what we beheld and our hands handled . . . we proclaim to you also" (1 John 1:1, 3).

Besides the Twelve, Paul rightfully claimed apostleship because Jesus had revealed Himself and had spoken directly to him (Gal. 1:1; Eph. 1:1; Col. 1:1). Paul's unique call and commission formed the basis of his authority among the churches (Acts 9).

Barnabas, Silas, Timothy, and lesser-known men, such as Andronicus and Junias (Rom. 16:7), constitute a secondary group of apostles. They were apostles of the church, but not directly commissioned by the risen Lord.

The Foundation of Doctrine

The apostles fulfilled a specific purpose in God's plan. The church was "built upon the foundation of the apostles and prophets" (Eph. 2:20). The mystery of the church was also revealed through the "holy apostles and prophets in the Spirit" (3:5). The apostles preached the truth that became the foundation of Christian doctrine ("the apostles' teaching," Acts 2:42). Those gifted men affirmed God's truth authoritatively, based on the Old Testament Scriptures and what they had witnessed of Christ's teachings, death, and resurrection. God authenticated their teaching "by signs and wonders and by various miracles" (Heb. 2:4), and with "the signs of a true apostle" (2 Cor. 12:12).

In the scriptural history of the early church, as recorded in Acts, the last time the apostles met as a body was at the Council of Jerusalem (Acts 15). After that, except for John, Paul, and Paul's fellowlaborers, they don't appear in Scripture except by brief mention in some of the epistles. As the gospel spread and churches were founded, leadership fell to faithful believers who followed the apostolic teaching. The apostles planted churches and taught new believers in the faith, but gradually local elders supplanted the founders. The tiny assemblies began to operate for themselves. As the church grew, members of the original foundation faded from literal view.

Paul does not refer to Old Testament prophets but to New Testament ones in Ephesians 4. They were another temporary group of gifted believers given to the infant church (see Eph. 2:20; 3:5). Since the New Testament did not yet exist, these prophets complemented the apostles and spoke directly from God.

The prophets' role as spokespersons posed a potential problem. Prophets could conceivably speak something as authoritative that was actually their own idea. For this reason Paul ordered that "the spirits of prophets are subject to prophets" (1 Cor. 14:32). They were to check on one another during the course of their ministries (14:29).

Such prophetic ministry ceased with the writing of the New Testament. Today God doesn't speak to the church by direct revelation through individuals. His "direct revelation" is in the words of Scripture, inspired by the Holy Spirit, inerrant and authoritative for the believer. God's revelation in the Bible is complete, and His written Word emphatically warns against adding to it or subtracting from it (Rev. 22:18-19). If believers want to know God's revelation today, they need to read and study the Bible.

The New Testament picture of an evangelist is of a man who goes from place to place where the gospel has not been preached. He preaches Christ and leads people to faith in Him. He teaches the resulting believers basic doctrine, stays until they mature, then appoints elders, and finally moves on to the next place. The New Testament-style evangelist is not a man who comes to town for a week of meetings and then leaves. His work isn't finished until he has planted a church. Timothy and Philip are examples.

Protecting the Body

The office of pastor-teacher is one, not two. The idea is of a teaching shepherd for the church, who stays in one place teaching the gospel and sound doctrine, while at the same time pastoring the sheep. The pastor-teacher takes over when the evangelist leaves.

The teaching shepherds' main task is to protect the flock. They are to protect it both from dangerous places and from enemies. They do this by building safeguards, teaching the truth, and helping those who may be stumbling into sin. They not only preserve them, but also strengthen and encourage them. Jesus, of course, is the chief Shepherd. He loves His flock and builds His church.

The Body needs to recognize God's plan. In some churches, leadership is removed from gifted believers in the name of spontaneity and freedom of the Spirit. But it is a serious error to think, "We'll just get together and see how the Spirit leads."

In God's plan for the Body, the Holy Spirit does not have primary responsibility for church order or the planning of services. In fact, the church at Corinth encountered problems because of an apparent failure by the gifted leaders. The believers tried to do their own thing, and this reaped chaos and confusion. So Paul rebuked them and reminded them that God is not the author of confusion (1 Cor. 14:23-24).

Order in the local church is the responsibility of the gifted believers who lead it. Without careful guidance from the leadership, whenever that order is set loose, the chances are great that some people who are not Spirit-led will attempt to lead. What occurs then may be more sociological and psychological than biblical. The results are uncertain, confusing, and perhaps even demonic.

Even though church planters and teaching shepherds have replaced apostles and prophets in the Body, the task is the same: to bring believers to maturity. Their task is not to fill the building, but to equip the saints.

This passion for maturity in the Body is a prominent New

Testament theme. Paul told the Colossians, "We proclaim Him, admonishing every man and teaching every man with all wisdom, that we may present every man complete in Christ" (1:28). Paul would settle for nothing less than maturity in his converts.

Then there was Epaphras, "a bondslave of Jesus Christ . . . always laboring earnestly for you in his prayers, that you may stand *perfect* and *fully assured* in all the will of God" (4:12; emphasis added). Epaphras is not famous like Paul, but he prayed passionately that every member of the Body would reach maturity. This is always to be the passion of gifted leaders. The call to the ministry is not a call to a profession, but to a passion. God gives gifted leaders to the church—not to entertain it, program it, or organize it—but to bring believers to maturity. Nothing less satisfies God's chosen leaders (Heb. 13:20-21; James 1:4).

How do the divinely gifted leaders of God build up the saints to maturity in the local church today? The answer is found in Paul's words to Timothy: "Preach the word; be ready in season and out of season; reprove, rebuke, exhort, with great patience and instruction" (2 Tim. 4:2). The Prophet Hosea said, "My people are destroyed for lack of knowledge" (Hosea 4:6). The Word of God must be taught to renew the mind before the Christian life can become mature (Rom. 12:2; Eph. 4:23).

Elsewhere Paul instructed Timothy on the value of God's Word for teaching: "All Scripture is inspired by God and profitable for teaching, for reproof, for correction, for training in righteousness; that the man of God may be adequate, equipped for every good work" (2 Tim. 3:16-17).

Timothy's job was to transmit the things he learned to faithful leaders, who in turn could teach others (2 Tim. 2:2). This pattern is still God's plan, and it works in the ministry today: teach believers the Word of God, who will teach others, who will in turn teach others. Experiential maturity of the members of the Body develops through the Word of God. (Of course, the pastor-teacher must be a "workman" in the Word [2 Tim. 2:15] in order to teach it effectively to the Body.)

The basic directive in Ephesians 4:12, "the equipping of the saints," is the heart of the pastor's ministry. Anything less is a perversion. Spending time on other things is to miss God's basic calling. The pastor's heart should throb with the same motives and actions Paul had: "We night and day keep praying most earnestly that we may see your face, and may complete what is lacking in your faith" (1 Thes. 3:10).

One of the tenderest scenes recorded in the Bible took place the day Paul left Ephesus, after three years of building up the believers there. Every evangelist and teaching pastor should prayerfully study this account (Acts 20:17-38). In it Paul characterizes his ministry in simple terms: "*Teaching* you publicly and from house to house. . . . I did not shrink from declaring to you *the whole purpose* of God" (Acts 20:20, 27; emphasis added).

Paul had systematically taught Bible doctrine to the Ephesian church. Now he was leaving that responsibility to the elders, the teaching pastors, who would remain. He sets forth the reasons for this commission: the value of the church to God, the inevitability of false teachers moving in with perverse dogma, and the inability of anything else to build up the saints to maturity.

The response to his farewell speaks in the most beautiful way of how believers will respond if God's teachers properly teach them: "And when he had said these things, he knelt down and prayed with them all. And they began to weep aloud and embraced Paul, and repeatedly kissed him, grieving especially over the word which he had spoken" (vv. 36-38).

It was his "word"—the instruction in doctrine—that endeared Paul most to the Ephesian elders. The people of God need the Word of God, and when it is given and bears fruit in their lives, their gratitude is a sweet reward to the teacher.

Teaching Believers

The second stage in the progress to maturity is what believers themselves do: "For the equipping of the saints *for the work of service*" (Eph. 4:12, emphasis added). These gifted pastors are to teach the Word to equip the saints to do the work. Teaching is the pastor's main job. Receiving the Word and ministering it so the Body may grow are mainly tasks for the members.

Too often, however, members of the flock who expect pastors to do everything thwart this biblical pattern. No wonder some pastors suffer so much physical and emotional fatigue. They can't find the time to study the Word of God because their members expect them not only to equip the saints, but also to do the work of the ministry.

An incident in the early church well illustrates God's plan. A dispute arose because certain widows were being neglected in the daily dispensing of food. The apostles resolved the matter with a significant decision. They told the church to appoint seven Spirit-filled men to look after the distribution of food, because "we will devote ourselves to prayer, and to the ministry of the Word" (Acts 6:4).

The apostles were not being proud or lazy. They were not above menial work or visiting people. But they had established a priority for their own ministry. They knew God's plan for the church. As divinely gifted men, their distinct contribution to the Body was praying and teaching the Word to equip the saints for the ministry.

The apostles also recognized that the Body needs all its members. There is a "work of service" for each to perform. In fact, these parallel ministries of gifted leaders and members of the Body show that the modern functional split between clergy and laity is a false one. It destroys the beauty of the Body. The gifted leaders given to the church are no better than the individual members; in God's plan He simply chose some to have the privilege of preaching and teaching. Having that role in the plan of God does not elevate them qualitatively, but it also doesn't require them to be looking after a host of details unrelated to their primary task. The dynamic of the early church came from a proper understanding of roles in the Body: gifted leaders building up the saints, who in turn exercise spiritual ministries throughout the Body. No part of the Body was seen as greater than the other, but each believer fulfilled his or her calling.

We need to define this "work of service, to the building up of the body of Christ" (Eph. 4:12) that believers are called on to perform. There are many church activities that cannot legitimately be called spiritual ministries, even though they are useful to the church program. This is not to minimize any activity—even putting up posters, for that matter—but it is to emphasize that the publicity chairperson should also have a personal, spiritual ministry in the building up of the Body. That is the kind of service Paul is speaking of in verse 12.

Exercising Gifts

God has given each member certain spiritual gifts (see also chap. 8 of this book) for the work of the ministry. These gifts can be exercised in many ways: visiting the sick and shut-ins; counseling new Christians; praying and studying the Bible with others; taking food, clothes, and money to people in special need; showing personal love and care for the lonely and discouraged; and reaching out to neighbors and friends with the gospel.

The local church essentially is a training ground to equip Christians to carry out their own ministries. Unfortunately, however, many believers view their local church as a place to go to watch paid professionals perform and carry out the church program. In many quarters Christianity has deteriorated into a professional "pulpitism" and a spiritual entertainment and service enterprise financed by lay spectators.

This scheme is not only a violation of God's plan, but also an absolute detriment to the growth of the church and the vitality of the members of the Body. Every member needs to find a significant place of service. To limit the work of the ministry to a small, select class of full-time "Christian workers" hinders the spiritual growth of God's people, stunts the discipleship process in the Body, and lessens the evangelistic outreach of the church into the community.

From the members who give themselves to the work of the ministry, God Himself will choose certain ones to be His gifts to the whole church. This is a never-ending cycle. Every congregation ought to be producing faithful workers, some of whom will be called by God to become full-time evangelists and pastor-teachers. That is exactly what happened in Philip's life. His ministry began as a Spirit-filled deacon in Jerusalem (Acts 6:5), and then God called him to a wider evangelistic ministry (Acts 8:5-40). Those called by God will then be used by Him to train others, and from those God will in turn call more gifted ones. This ongoing process is basic to His plan for the maturation of the Body.

I am more and more committed to the proposition that each local church ought to be developing its own spiritual leadership rather than bringing in outsiders to be leaders. If a church is not producing

competent leaders to serve Christ in a full-time capacity, something
is wrong.

At Grace Community Church our gifted evangelists and pastor-
teachers have come from within the ranks of the congregation. God
has brought them to maturity by His Spirit, through His Word. These
people were "faithful in a little," and God gave them a larger
responsibility. The result for our church has been a unique quality of unity, fellowship, and commitment to each other—leaders and
flock alike. Such an atmosphere is more difficult to achieve if the
ministering staff is assembled from outside the congregation. The
first level of my ministry has been to "disciple" our gifted men. Our
staff has grown from the soil of much time that we have spent with
each one in personal fellowship, teaching, and prayer. Some have
matured to the point that they have been sent out to mission fields
and other churches.

In fact, though we pray and work for souls to be saved, we have
never deliberately sought more people to swell our attendance num-
bers. We have no right to ask God for more people until we see progress
in those He has already given us to equip. Thank God, there has
been progress. We see the saints feeding and loving each other, counseling each other, caring for each other, nourishing each other, and
even developing, organizing, and operating various ministries
within the church.

I remember once seeing, at a circus, a man spinning plates on eight
sticks. He would get all eight going and have to run back to keep
the first one spinning, and so on up and down the line. This seems
to me an apt illustration of the role of pastors who have figured out
the plates they want to spin and who look through the congregation to find the right sticks. They get everything going and discover
that the sticks by themselves don't keep the plates moving, so
they must run up and down from plate to plate and assist the fal-
tering sticks. How much better it is for pastors to concentrate all
their efforts on "the equipping of the saints" so that as believers grow
they begin certain ministries that interest them and are on their hearts.
Well-equipped saints will, out of energy and excitement, develop
ministries within the church.

The Results of Maturity

As a result, the Body of Christ is built up (Eph. 4:12). When each member performs his or her ministry, the whole Body comes to maturity. And Paul specifies five results of this entire maturation process (vv. 13-15).

"Unity of the Faith" (Eph. 4:13)

If gifted leaders equip the saints, and the saints do the work of the ministry, the Body grows and believers are united. If sometimes there is a breakdown, it is because either the pastor doesn't adequately teach the Word to equip the believers or the believers do not accept their responsibility of ministry.

Because the whole Body is affected, it disturbs me to see pastors and evangelists who are not teaching the Word. They have active programs, but their busy schedules crowd out study of the Word, and they don't teach it in every service.

"They were continually devoting themselves to the apostles' teaching and to fellowship, to the breaking of bread and to prayer" (Acts 2:42). This is our biblical pattern for the preservation of unity in the Body. "And the congregation of those who believed were of one heart and soul; and not one of them claimed that anything belonging to him was his own; but all things were common property to them" (4:32).

Those members of the early Jerusalem church also had great boldness and power in their witness to Christ. They won people to Him every day (2:47).

Because they gave themselves to the study of the Word and ministered to one another, their love and unity had a profound impact on the world. If the Body is to be one, it cannot break down at any point.

"The Knowledge of the Son of God" (Eph. 4:13)

Some Christians' knowledge of Christ is limited to His saving work on their behalf. In God's purpose, however, we are to grow in more intimate fellowship with our Lord and Savior. The church that is learning and serving will be deeply involved with Jesus Christ. The maturing Christian experiences an increasingly richer personal fellowship with the Son of God.

Becoming More like Jesus Christ

This results from the deeper, more intimate fellowship with Him that we just mentioned. Paul describes the believer's goal: "to a mature man" (Eph. 4:13). The word implies a fully developed, robust, spiritually healthy person. God is not satisfied when we accept anything less for our standard. Of course, the perfect example of the mature man is Christ. No one has arrived spiritually until he or she attains Christ's stature. Once in a while we think we have made great spiritual strides, but lest we think there's no further to go, Paul keeps the standard before us: "the fulness of Christ" (v. 13).

It's easy, of course, to stop at some lower level, but the progressively maturing believer will settle for nothing less than the fullness of Christ. We must constantly strive to be like Jesus in everything we do, not just to claim some spiritual achievement, but because we want to show our love and reverence for Christ. As this kind of believer, we will want to be like Christ because we love Him.

One day when my son Mark was small, I asked him what he wanted to be when he grew up.

"I'm going to be a dad, just like you," he said.

"Well, why do you want to be a dad just like me?" I asked him.

"Because I love you," he said.

He wanted to be like me because he loves and respects me. Since I am the object of his love as his father, he wanted to emulate me.

Solid in Doctrine

"As a result, we are no longer to be children, tossed here and there by waves, and carried about by every wind of doctrine, by the trickery of men, by craftiness in deceitful scheming" (Eph. 4:14).

Children are gullible and undiscerning. They don't know what's good or bad. Give them a choice of diet, and they'll eat what tastes good but has no nutritional value. Children will believe anyone. God's purpose in bringing His children to maturity is so they will not act like gullible, undiscerning children when it comes to doctrine. They are not to be susceptible to every new religious fad. They are to be strong, firm, confident of what they believe—not tossed about by the shifting winds of ungodly philosophies.

Some Christians, because they are spiritual babies, fall victim to false teaching. But if we submit ourselves to solid, balanced, scriptural teaching, and give ourselves to spiritual ministry, error will not sway us. Rather than being thrown off by error, we will be able to expose it. God's will is for every believer to grow up out of spiritual childhood and so not be susceptible when crafty deceivers come around.

In fact, the Apostle John speaks of levels of spiritual growth (1 John 2:13-14). The second level, "young men," is those who conquer Satan ("the evil one"). Since Satan's major effort is in false doctrine (see 2 Cor. 11:14), it indicates that only those who have spiritually grown from babies to young adults can deal with erroneous teaching.

"Speaking the Truth in Love" (Eph. 4:15)

The climax is the proclamation of God's truth, in love, by every believer, both to other believers and to unbelievers. This is the end result for the Christian who really knows Christ, who wants to be like Him, and who is strong in faith and doctrine. Proclaiming the truth is the believer's work of service, something we can do in our communities and in our workplaces.

God's plan, then, for building up the Body is progressive. He gives gifted leaders to the church to equip the saints. Thus the saints are equipped to do the work of the ministry. The Body grows, becomes mature, and comes together in unity. Individual members have a deep, abiding fellowship with Christ and grow in His likeness. They know sound doctrine, combat false teaching, and go into the community with a dynamic, loving presentation of the gospel.

In discussing the maturation of the believer in the Body, it is easy to get the impression that everything depends on us. True, Scripture clearly outlines human responsibility—gifted leaders are to teach, and the saints are to respond and grow. But if that were the end of the matter, bringing the Body to maturity would be just another humanistic scheme. Such a conclusion could not be further from the truth.

Notice what the remainder of Ephesians 4:15 and all of verse 16 says: "We are to grow up in all aspects into Him, who is the Head, even Christ, from whom the whole body, being fitted and held together by that which every joint supplies, according to the proper working of each individual part, causes the growth of the body for the building up of itself in love." The Body's growth is from Jesus Christ. He is the source of the power to make the progress and purposes of maturation actually happen. And this power source will be unleashed only when the Word of God is faithfully proclaimed to the Body, and the members of the Body do the work of the ministry.

7

The Unity of the Body

The human body is an amazing organism. God created it to be extremely complex. Yet it is unequaled in its degree of harmony and interrelatedness. If one part is cut off or ceases to function, or even if a part is just impaired, the rest of the body suffers a loss of effectiveness. It is designed to work together as a unit.

The Body of Christ is also one. There are many denominations, a lot of Christian organizations, and all sorts of agencies, clubs, and groups. But there is only one true church, and everyone who has genuinely come to Jesus Christ in repentance and faith is a member. Undergirding all scriptural teaching about the Body of Christ is this concept of *oneness* or *unity:* "For even as the body is one and yet has many members, and all the members of the body, though they are many, are one body, so also is Christ" (1 Cor. 12:12).

A physical body is made up of members functioning together. Your hand is not so gifted that you can cut it off and send it to do a job alone. The hand would then no longer be skilled at anything—it would die. Thus the essence of the body is unity.

In the church body, Christ is the Head, and the Head is the life. Continuing the analogy between the physical body and the church, you can cut off a hand or an arm and maintain life, but if you cut off the head, the body's life is gone. The same is true in the Body of Christ. Believers are one in Christ and receive all spiritual life and resources—strength, wisdom, and instructions—from the same head.

Paul refers to "one body" three times to emphasize Body unity (vv. 12-13). Christians are one. Salvation is the initial point of unity. Christians are united because they are all baptized by one Spirit into one Body.

People often ask, "What is the baptism of the Holy Spirit?" It is simply God's Spirit placing a believer into the Body of Christ: "By one Spirit we were all baptized into one body" (v. 13). We come into the Body of Christ at the moment of our salvation, being placed there by the energy of the Holy Spirit. The Spirit not only places believers into the Body, but He also indwells each one of us.

There is no such thing as a believer who doesn't have the Holy Spirit: "If anyone does not have the Spirit of Christ, he does not belong to Him" (Rom. 8:9). Paul reminded the Ephesians "to preserve the unity of the Spirit in the bond of peace" (Eph. 4:3), because the same Spirit who regenerates Christians and baptizes them into the Body also indwells them.

One in the Spirit

The church's unity, therefore, is not based on an artificial, organizational relationship. Nor on the fact that people are churchgoers. Rather, all believers have been identified in the work of a single Spirit. We are one in the Spirit.

Even though Christians have been given this oneness, they have a tendency to pull apart and isolate themselves into smaller "like-minded" subgroups. It's possible for Christians to go to the same church meetings, sit together, and even talk superficially, but at heart still be far from one another. Most believers are not open to one another and have not learned to express oneness in practical ways. This is contrary to the way the church is supposed to function, and as a result the whole Body is hindered. Much of today's pastoral ministry involves getting Christians to realize their oneness and to put it into practice.

No hierarchy is expressed in the Body metaphor. There are varying gifts within the church, but there is no structure that accentuates superior and inferior positions. The organizational chart of Christianity is simple—Christ, the head of the Body. There are levels of authority (1 Tim. 5:17), but that is not to be equated with spiritual superiority. Leaders are not some kind of upper-division Christians.

Every biblical metaphor of the church, without exception, emphasizes its unity. The church is one Bride with one husband; one Flock with one shepherd; the Branches on one vine; one Kingdom with one king; one Family with one father; one Building with one foundation; one Body with one head. Each of these illustrations involves a group related to the same perfect leader, Jesus Christ. *Positionally*, each believer stands on the same ground in Christ.

There is no such thing as an isolated believer—one who is by himself or herself and not part of the Body. Whether babies, "young men," or mature "fathers" spiritually (1 John 2:12-14), whether weak or strong (1 Cor. 3:16), Christians are one (1 John 2:12-14).

The Apostle Paul had to work with a church at Corinth that was badly split (1 Cor. 1:12). Some members said, "I am an Apollos follower." Others said, "Well, not me. I'm a Paul follower." "You're both wrong! Cephas is in," some said. Then the really pious ones spoke up, "Listen, folks, I follow Christ" (v. 12). Paul replied to all this, "Has Christ been divided?" (v. 13) "Let no one boast in men" (3:21). Christians cannot say, "I follow him, or I follow that one." The apostle adds, "For all things belong to you, whether Paul or Apollos or Cephas or the world or life or death or things present or things to come, all things belong to you, and you belong to Christ; and Christ belongs to God" (vv. 21-23).

Christians are to end their party bickering and return to the oneness of a redeemed people. After all, they owe that distinct unity to having been brought into one Body by one Spirit and having been indwelt by the same Spirit.

Becoming Like Christ

The New Testament word for church is *ekklesia*, which means "assembly" and is from a verb meaning "to call out." Christians are called apart from the world to exist as a distinct entity. They are to lead lives worthy of that divine calling (Eph. 4:1), so that they may become in character and conduct what they are by virtue of their union with Christ. The Christian life is the process of working out in practice the spiritual resources of the believer's position in Christ.

> You were at that time separate from Christ, excluded from the commonwealth of Israel, and strangers to the covenants of promise, having no hope and without God in the world. But now in Christ Jesus you who formerly were far off have been brought near by the blood of Christ. For He Himself is our peace, who made both groups into one, and broke down the barrier of the dividing wall, by abolishing in His flesh the enmity . . . that in Himself He might make the two into one new man, thus establishing peace, and might reconcile them both in one body to God through the cross. . . . for through Him we both have our access in one Spirit to the Father (2:12-16, 18).

There is to be no partiality in the church. Christ has abolished the barriers of nationality, race, class, and sex to make all believers one. Paul further underscores this point, "There is neither Jew nor Greek, there is neither slave nor free man, there is neither male nor female, for you are all one in Christ Jesus" (Gal. 3:28).

Some people, however, have a hard time accepting this fact and allowing it to control their lives. They don't realize that in Christ all discrimination ends. The church that Christ has created, of which He is Head, tolerates no racial distinctions.

A number of years ago I was involved in a special evangelistic effort among African Americans of one community. My team was constantly under police surveillance. At one point we were arrested and fined, accused of stirring up the blacks. Then we were threatened with a public beating if we didn't stop our meetings. The chief of police was especially profane and abusive. I told him we were in the town only to preach Jesus Christ and asked him if he objected to that. He said he didn't and added that he himself was a Sunday School superintendent! Although we were released, we were constantly watched until the mission was over.

The attitudes of some of the people in that town and that church were not scriptural. They were not seeing the truth of Romans 10:12-13, which says, "For there is no distinction between Jew and Greek; for the same Lord is Lord of all, abounding in riches for all who call upon Him; for 'Whoever will call upon the name of the Lord will be saved.'"

THE UNITY OF THE BODY

Attaining unity was especially difficult in the early church because of the separation between Jews and Gentiles. Jesus, however, abolished the hostility between Jews and Gentiles created by the Law. The Jews were intent on keeping the Law, and they glorified themselves for doing so; at the same time, they looked down on those who didn't. The Gentile, therefore, was considered an outcast. But when Jesus died on the cross, He did away with external law-keeping as a testimony to faith. The Gentile no longer was excluded from the fullness of all God's blessings.

Scripture says the Law was good in that it revealed God's holiness and human sinfulness. When Jesus died, He fully accepted the punishment due sinners for lawbreaking, but at the same time He met all the Law's demands. The Law, therefore, could make no more claims on Jew or Gentile. And if the Law no longer keeps people from God, it doesn't separate us from one another. If Jew and Gentile were to be brought together, the enmity mentioned in Ephesians 2:15 had to be abolished. That's what happened when Jesus died and rose from the dead. In place of the old animosity, Christ created "one new man."

No Distinctions in the Body

In France during World War II, some GIs took the body of a buddy to a local cemetery. They were stopped by a priest, who said, "Sorry, boys, you can't bury your friend here if he's not a Catholic." Though discouraged, the GIs didn't give up; they decided to bury him outside the cemetery fence. Next morning when they went to pay their last respects at the grave, they couldn't find it. After looking for an hour, they asked the priest about it. He explained, "Well, the first part of the night I stayed awake, sorry for what I had told you. The second part of the night I spent moving the fence."

Jesus, in effect, moved the fence and included every believer from every nation in God's promises, which are received by faith apart from the works of the Law. This means there is no reason for Christians not to love one another. Christ has removed man-made ethnic barriers within His Body.

Paul in his writings calls Christians fellow heirs, fellow members, fellow partakers, and fellow citizens. All these terms emphasize the unity of the Body. Christians, therefore, are not to cut themselves off from fellow believers. Rather, their responsibility is to move into the mainstream of Body life. Some Christians, when they go to church, just sit, as if to say, "Well, God, I know You're really blessed by my being here." They don't know what it means to live in the vitality and nourishment received from Christ's Body. In effect, though sharing the same identity by virtue of their faith, they do not share the same practice. They weaken the Body. Such Christians' failure to grow in their commitment affects everyone, because other believers try to compensate for what those members fail to contribute.

Jesus wanted all believers to experience unity. And so He prayed to His Father, "I do not ask in behalf of these alone [the disciples], but for those also who believe in Me through their word; that they may all be one; even as Thou, Father, art in Me, and I in Thee, that they also may be in Us; that the world may believe that Thou didst send Me. And the glory which Thou hast given Me I have given to them; that they may be one, just as We are one" (John 17:20-22).

His glory is the Holy Spirit (1 Peter 4:14), and the presence of the Holy Spirit is the believer's point of unity. "I in them, and Thou in Me, that they may be perfected in unity, that the world may know that Thou didst send Me, and didst love them, even as Thou didst love Me" (John 17:23).

The Keys to Unity

When are Christians going to turn this world upside down? When are they going to shatter its complacency? When they experience oneness! If a local congregation begins to minister to the needs of each member with supersensitive unity, the world will be astounded with the results. That church will release the unity and energy of the Holy Spirit and begin to reach people in its community.

Humility
Christians are to have the mind of Christ "who, although He existed in the form of God, did not regard equality with God a thing to be grasped, but emptied Himself, taking the form of a bond-ser-

vant, and being made in the likeness of men. And being found in appearance as a man, He humbled Himself by becoming obedient to the point of death, even death on a cross" (Phil. 2:6-8). The mind of Christ is *humility*. "Do not merely look out for your own personal interests, but also for the interests of others" (v. 4).

Can you imagine what would happen if all Christians cared more for others than themselves? All Christians would get the care they need, because all would have someone caring for them. This is the mind of humility. But unfortunately, many Christians spend so much time on themselves that no one can tolerate caring for them. Such self-centered believers are often more concerned about their egos being offended than they are about serving others.

Christ never tried to maintain His ego. Mockers spat on Him, and He just stood there. His enemies wanted to nail Him to a cross, and He allowed them to, without a word of protest. The mind of humility says, "If this means your salvation and your benefit and blessing, I'll suffer because I care about you." That attitude is foreign to much of contemporary Christian experience, but it is what the Body concept is all about.

Selfless Paul exhibited Christlike humility: "But even if I am being poured out as a drink-offering upon the sacrifice and service of your faith, I rejoice" (v. 17). He was expendable for the sake of others. And he exhorts us, "For through the grace given to me I say to every man among you not to think more highly of himself than he ought to think. . . . For just as we have many members in one body" (Rom. 12:3-4). All Christians experience unity by humbly thinking about others instead of themselves, and then reaching out to serve someone else.

Should humility go so far that Christians allow themselves to get trampled? Yes, if necessary; God can restore us. Paul condemns a Christian who sues another Christian, goes to court, and hassles publicly with the other believer. "Actually, then, it is already a defeat for you, that you have lawsuits with one another. Why not rather be wronged? Why not rather be defrauded? On the contrary, you yourselves wrong and defraud, and that your brethren" (1 Cor. 6:7-8).

Paul says Christians are to care so much for each other that they are less concerned about what happens to themselves. A brother in Christ may be defrauded, but another Christian should pick him up, because a caring person often gets back the love he or she gives. Paul adds that if he dies in ministering to others, that is only "gain" (see Phil. 1:21). Each of us is expendable for the other.

Love

Along with humility, love is needed to experience Christian oneness. "A new commandment I give to you, that you love one another" (John 13:34). This love for the other believer is not selective, neither is it based on that person's attractiveness. It doesn't depend on circumstances, neither is it linked to what the other person does.

Sometimes one believer will say of another, "I love her in the Lord." This is the same as saying, "I hate her." It's as if a Christian had a little valve and squirted the other believer with a few drops of divine love, unmixed with his or her own, and then shut off the valve. But, in truth, either we love another believer or we don't. Jesus said love is not an option, but a new commandment. Christians don't have a natural capacity to love everyone, but "the love of God has been poured out within our hearts" (Rom. 5:5).

How are Christians to love? Jesus continues His command in John 13: "Even as I have loved you, that you also love one another. By this all men will know that you are My disciples, if you have love for one another" (vv. 34-35). Christ had just shown love to the disciples by washing their feet. Such love is not an emotion, but an act of selfless, sacrificial service to meet someone's need.

Christians can convince the world that Jesus is real by loving one another as He prescribed. The greatest evangelism is not having a big revival; it is having so much love that the world can't figure it out. Paul prayed, "May the Lord cause you to increase and abound in love for one another" (1 Thes. 3:12).

The love that characterizes Christian unity causes one believer to go to his brother and say, "Brother, I have held bitterness against you, and I want to ask you to forgive me. I want to begin to love you." In response to that or any other specific apology, concern for church unity says, "Brother, I forgive you."

If you have genuine love, you won't criticize others to build up yourself. You will love no matter the cost—whether in money, prestige, or position.

Diversity

The church is not only unified but also diversified—Christians are one and yet they are many: "For the body is not one member, but many" (1 Cor. 12:14).

The human body is one, and yet there are arms, fingers, and all the various parts and organs, each with unique functions, operating distinctly, and yet as one. Similarly, there *is diversity* within the Body of Christ—Christians are all different individuals.

God has given Christians different gifts, and the measure of faith to go with each gift. In other words, He provides sufficient faith to exercise the various spiritual gifts. Christians need to complement one another; no one can be or do everything. I am gifted to do one thing, someone else to do another, and we minister to one another for the Body's health. Remember, any member who doesn't function cripples the whole Body.

The Body of Christ, then, is marked by unity *with* diversity. "There are varieties of effects, but the same God who works all things in all persons. . . . But one and the same Spirit works all these things, distributing to each one individually just as He wills" (vv. 6, 11). So that all believers may minister to one another, the Spirit has apportioned gifts in beautiful balance. As all believers are being ministered to and are ministering their gifts, they all are maturing and working together as one Body.

Football players know the validity of the unity with diversity principle. Each player must carry out his assignment if the team is going to win. Imagine a player asserting in an interview that the team is one, really one—so much "one" that everyone has decided to play quarterback. That's not unity; it's chaos. The football team doesn't need eleven quarterbacks. There must be diversity in the midst of basic harmony. The team needs ends, tackles, guards, a center, and backs. Each player must be fully committed to his unique place on the team if there's to be unity. My coach used to say, "If you believe that your position is the most important one on the field, and if you play it that way on every play, we can't be beaten!"

Diversity is vital to the functioning of the church. Spiritual gifts are sovereign, God-given blessings, and believers must use the one or ones they have received. There are many opportunities within the church program and outside it to exercise gifts. If a Christian has the gift of helps, for example, that believer may find someone in his or her church or his or her neighborhood who needs help. If a Christian has the gift of teaching, that believer may exercise it with an entire Sunday School class or with only one or two children in his or her neighborhood. Needs are so great that all Christians can minister their gifts and are without excuse if they do not.

Therefore, a believer doesn't necessarily need the structured organization of the local church to minister his or her gifts. I've told my congregation, "You who are working here in the church, this is where God has put you—use your gifts. But if you find no opening, if there is no place for you to minister within the church program, go and minister to someone outside."

Harmony

The Body of Christ must also have *harmony* in the ministering of gifts:

> If the foot should say, "Because I am not a hand, I am not a part of the body," it is not for this reason any the less a part of the body. And if the ear should say, "Because I am not an eye, I am not part of the body," it is not for this reason any the less a part of the body. If the whole body were an eye, where would the hearing be? If the whole were hearing, where would the sense of smell be? But now God has placed the members, each one of them, in the body, just as He desired. And if they were all one member, where would the body be? But now there are many members, but one body. And the eye cannot say to the hand, "I have no need of you"; or again the head to the feet, "I have no need of you." On the contrary, it is much truer that the members of the body which seem to be weaker are necessary; and those members of the body, which we deem less honorable, on these we bestow more abundant honor, and our unseemly members come to have more abundant seemliness, whereas our seemly members have no need of it. But God has so composed the body, giving more abundant honor to that member which lacked, that there should be no division in the body, but that the members should have the same care for one another (1 Cor. 12:15-25).

This passage expresses the Christian's attitude of respect for each fellow member. All Christians are to be content with their gifts and are to harmonize with the whole Body. It is not always the most obvious gift that is most critical. A beautiful head of hair is nice, but an ugly lung is essential.

In the Body of Christ there should be unity, diversity, and harmony. To be a healthy body, the church needs every Christian doing his or her part—not necessarily more structure or organization. In other words, the church needs more unity and more ministry. Indeed, Jesus prayed for this in John 17.

Christian unity is the unity of the Spirit, not of the denomination or the organization. There will be true Body unity when Christians humble themselves, when they work for the interests of others, when they love with selfless love, and when they minister their gifts in harmony.

The Gifts of the Body

G od wants to reach the whole world with His truth.
Therefore, the Holy Spirit has specially empowered
and enabled members of the Body to carry out some very
important functions. In the Old Testament, Israel was God's vehi-
cle to reach the world. In the New Testament era, Jesus and His disciples were God's vehicles. Today God uses the church to communicate
to the world His nature and His truth.

The church's witness is not only verbal or merely a communication
of the gospel in specifics, but it is also the witness of love and unity.
When believers are one in love, the world will find their witness impres-
sive. A unity, built on humility and love, becomes the church's greatest testimony. Though believers have been made one by the Holy
Spirit's placing them into the Body of Christ, and though they are
all indwelt by the same Holy Spirit, the world usually does not see
them as one in practice. Christians today do not have a singular testimony of humility and love.

Satan wants the church to be divided. While the prayer of Christ
was that Christians be one, and while the activity of the Holy
Spirit is to make them one, all of the energy of Satan is to fracture
Christian unity. Whenever a divisive issue arises within the Body
of Christ, we can be sure one side is the agent of Satan. Christ wants
to unify; Satan wants to divide. There are so many disobedient
Christians that Satan has been tremendously successful.

There is no scriptural justification for all the present divisions within the church. There were no denominations in the New Testament. In fact, church divisions are explicitly contrary to the teaching of the Word of God. Christ's intent in forming the Body was that believers be one, not divided into little parts.

The Body was formed in unity, not in discord. In the Book of Acts we read that the church began during a prayer meeting in the upper room of a house in Jerusalem. The disciples of Jesus had gathered there to pray (Acts 1:12-14). Out of their faith, obedience, and waiting in prayer, God brought into being the church (chap. 2). Men and women filled with the Holy Spirit and possessing His gifts went out of the room, into the streets, and preached Christ crucified and risen. They were humble people. There were no great ones. They had no organizational structure, but they "turned the world upside down" (17:6, KJV).

That was the birth of the church—the Body of Christ. It was accomplished in the energy of the Holy Spirit. From that time on, every member has been added to the church the same way—by the Spirit's placing us into the Body (1 Cor. 12:13). Christians are as organically one today as they were in Acts 2.

The early church was exciting. Believers were all filled with the Spirit and exercising their spiritual gifts. They were preaching the gospel, and people were added daily to the church. Believers had a unity of humble love that was manifest everywhere. The world was shaken, and people couldn't believe what was happening in Jerusalem.

For the church today to be an effective witness it must be as spiritually healthy as the early church. Not just organized, but also Spirit-filled. Not just supercommitted, but also exercising spiritual gifts. Not just giving out publicity, but also preaching the gospel. The standards have not changed. Christians must be mature, loving, and humble.

God's Plan for the Church

God wants the church to be powerful and functioning well. To accomplish that, He designed a plan for the church. Besides the gifted leaders given to the church (Eph. 4:11-12) to make it really grow and have a unified witness, God has given every member a certain function, or functions, to contribute to the health of the Body. The human body is an illustration of this. It has all kinds of organs that interact. If just one of those doesn't function, the whole body feels it. In the same way, every believer has a necessary ministry as a vital organ of the Body of Christ. Any believer's failure to serve cripples the Body to some degree.

Through the church, Christ wants to manifest His own character (v. 13). And He wants to do so through individual believers. To accomplish that, God gives every member a certain spiritual giftedness to minister to the rest of the Body.

Spiritual gifts are identified with Jesus Christ because, in their fullest sense, they were complete and perfectly operative in His preaching, teaching, and ministry to others. The reason God gives each believer differing gifts is that He wants the Body to manifest a composite Christlikeness. The gifts are not random; they are Christ's characteristics reproduced by the Spirit in the Body. That means the only way an individual Christian will ever be a person of full stature in Christ is when all the gifts are ministered to him or her.

That is why we must minister our gift to other believers. As we minister to others, we build them up in the area of that gift. If I as a pastor minister the gift of preaching, my people should learn how to communicate more effectively. If a believer in my church has the gift of showing mercy, and he or she ministers that gift to me, I not only receive the direct blessing and purpose of that gift, but I also learn a little more about how to show mercy. I may not have that gift, but I'm still built up in that area to some extent. As each member ministers to the other, all are built up as individuals to be like Christ and to show forth His attributes. Collectively, they manifest the total person of Christ. This is not meant to imply that all believers should minister all categories of gifts, nor that each Christian becomes a Body by himself or herself. But each is to reflect Christ.

The Definition of Spiritual Gifts

From 1 Corinthians 12 we learn the importance of spiritual gifts—their source, their power, and their extent. The importance of spiritual gifts is seen in Paul's opening statement, "Now concerning spiritual gifts, brethren, I do not want you to be unaware" (v. 1). Unfortunately, some believers are grossly unaware. Some abuse the spiritual gifts; others neglect them. Some Christians emphasize only the sign of miraculous gifts and ignore the edifying ones. But no congregation will be what the Holy Spirit gifted it and empowered it to be until it properly understands and exercises spiritual gifts.

The Holy Spirit is the source of spiritual gifts. "But one and the same Spirit works all these things [spiritual gifts], distributing to each one individually just as He wills" (v. 11). The day we were born into the family of God, the day that we received Jesus Christ as our personal Savior, the Spirit of God distributed to us a spiritual gift or gifts.

A spiritual gift is a channel through which the Holy Spirit ministers to the Body. A gift is not an end in itself. Every believer has a spiritual gift, regardless of his or her personal spiritual development. Therefore, possession of a spiritual gift does not mean a Christian is "spiritual." The question is whether or not the channel is clear. One conceivably might have all of the gifts recorded in Scripture, not be using them at all, or be abusing them. Such a believer would still be unspiritual. This was true of the assembly at Corinth (1 Cor. 1:7; 3:1-4).

Some people think they should seek certain gifts. They are told to "tarry" for certain gifts. Some even follow gimmicks and techniques to get them. They wrongly attempt to generate artificial, emotional, and even satanic activity, and then call such activity the gifts of the Spirit. The Holy Spirit, however, gives the gifts by divine will and divine choice. He knows what gifts are needed, where they are needed, when they are needed, and who is to receive what gifts.

It is also true that one can have a gift from the Holy Spirit and be doing nothing about it. Paul told Timothy, "Do not neglect the spiritual gift within you" (1 Tim. 4:14). Timothy had become sidetracked by certain people who were pressuring him and upsetting him. That stress contributed to his neglect of his spiritual gift. Evidently Timothy still wasn't doing too well later, prompting Paul to write, "I remind you to kindle afresh the gift of God which is in you" (2 Tim. 1:6).

A spiritual gift is not the same as a natural ability. You can't say,

"My gift is baking pies." That's a wonderful ability, but it is not a gift of the Spirit. Other believers might say, "My gift is to work with my hands," or "My gift is to sing." Those are not spiritual gifts; those are natural abilities. The spiritual gifts are sovereignly bestowed manifestations of the Spirit's power.

The Apostle Paul illustrates the difference between a spiritual gift and a natural ability. He obviously had natural ability to express himself publicly, but it is clear that he never regarded his ability to speak as a gift of the Spirit. He also was a man of tremendous learning. He could have used his knowledge of philosophy and literature to compose eloquent, convincing orations. He could have delivered them with magnificent ability. But instead he said this: "And when I came to you, brethren, I did not come with superiority of speech or of wisdom, proclaiming to you the testimony of God. For I determined to know nothing among you except Jesus Christ, and Him crucified" (1 Cor. 2:1-2).

The Holy Spirit expresses Himself through people. He uses human knowledge and ability, but in a supernatural way apart from the person's own ability.

Many people have the gift of gab, but they aren't necessarily preachers. If a believer has a natural aptitude for public speaking, perhaps the Holy Spirit will elect to use it; perhaps He won't.

On the other hand, I recall a friend in seminary who had a severe stuttering problem. My first reaction when I heard him in preaching class was, "There is no way that he belongs in the ministry as a preacher." Today he is a fine Bible teacher, an able expositor of the Word of God, and a lucid speaker, even though he still struggles with words. This man does not have a natural gift of eloquence, but he has the gift of preaching and teaching.

Thus God may elect to use a Christian's natural ability, or He may give us a spiritual gift that has no connection with our natural ability. Relying on natural ability for the production of spiritual fruit is a hindrance to what the Spirit wants to do. In 1 Peter 4:10-11 we read: "As each one has received a special gift, employ it in serving one another, as good stewards of the manifold grace of God. Whoever speaks, let him speak, as it were, the utterances of God; whoever serves, let him do so as by the strength which God supplies; so that in all things God may be glorified through Jesus Christ, to whom belongs the glory and dominion forever and ever. Amen." Notice that Peter says "special gift." This indicates a singular gift and is consistent with Paul's use of "the gift" (1 Tim. 4:14; 2 Tim. 1:6). I believe it indicates that each believer receives one gift, which is unique to him or her. But that gift may combine elements from all the categories of giftedness. Each believer is, then, a spiritual "snowflake"! This understanding also allows for the obvious diversity among believers.

In the Spirit or in the Flesh?

There is a difference between the natural ability to speak and the Spirit-given gift of preaching. However, it is possible for a person to have the gift of preaching, yet stand in the pulpit and preach in the flesh. I can verify, by personal experience, that it is a constant battle in my own heart and mind not to speak humanly, but to speak as the oracle of God and to bring my gifts into subjection to the Holy Spirit.

Having a spiritual gift doesn't necessarily mean one will always minister it in the Holy Spirit. "The spirits of prophets are subject to prophets" (1 Cor. 14:32). Even when we are called to be a preacher (prophet), we have to subject our spirit to other godly Christians. I am not spiritual just because I preach. The Apostle Paul says just that a few verses earlier, "Let two or three prophets speak, and let the others pass judgment" (v. 29). Since the prophets (those who preach and teach God's Word) are fallible, they must check each other to verify what they say. Spiritual gifts are no guarantee that a believer is always right.

In the flesh, a person can know nothing about the true nature of Christianity and spiritual gifts. Even something as basic as the lordship of Christ cannot be known unless the Holy Spirit reveals it. When Peter said to Jesus, "Thou art the Christ, the Son of the living God," Jesus replied, "Flesh and blood did not reveal this to you, but My Father who is in heaven" (Matt. 16:16-17).

Paul told his readers, "You know that when you were pagans, you were led astray to the dumb idols, however you were led" (1 Cor. 12:2).

The word "led" refers to leading a prisoner. The unsaved person is viewed in a kind of pathetic hopelessness, worshiping false gods who cannot speak because they do not exist. "Therefore I make known to you, that no one speaking by the Spirit of God says, 'Jesus is accursed'; and no one can say, 'Jesus is Lord,' except by the Holy Spirit" (v. 3).

To paraphrase Paul, "I don't want you to be ignorant about spiritual gifts, but you couldn't know about them because you don't know the basics. You couldn't know about spiritual gifts, until you knew the lordship of Christ, and you couldn't know that apart from the Holy Spirit." The flesh is incapable of knowing anything (2:10). If the natural man can't understand the lordship of Christ, how can he understand the work of the Holy Spirit through spiritual gifts? Spiritual understanding and spiritual work can be accomplished only by the power of the Spirit. That's why Jesus said, "You shall receive power when the Holy Spirit has come upon you" (Acts 1:8).

Whatever Christians do in their own flesh, in their own will and design, is a waste and mockery. But whatever they do by the Holy Spirit's power is borne along by divine energy. All a Christian needs to say is, "Spirit of God, use me," for divine energy to flow to the Body as he or she ministers. The Corinthian believers had the gifts, but through their immaturity and disobedience they had quenched and grieved the Holy Spirit.

There are three basic steps to using one's gift in the energy of the Spirit: *Prayer*—constantly ask God to cleanse your life and to use you in the Spirit's power; *Yield yourself to God*—resolve to continually live according to His will, not the world's (Rom. 6:16; 12:1-2); *Be filled with the Holy Spirit*—allow the Spirit of God to permeate every aspect of your life (Eph. 5:18). Turn every decision, thought, word, and action over to the Spirit's control. Commit all to Him.

Gifts That Build Up

God's Word indicates two kinds of spiritual gifts: permanent and temporary. Permanent gifts edify or build up the Body. These are the gifts that do not cease. They began in the early church and continue operating today. The temporary gifts, on the other hand, were not designed for edifying the Body, but were for confirming that *differ*

✳

⊀

the apostles' and prophets' words were from God. Scripture deals
in various places with four such gifts: miracles, healing, tongues, and
interpretation of tongues. They have no continuing role in the Body.
(For a full discussion of these gifts, see my book *Charismatic Chaos*
[Grand Rapids: Zondervan, 1992], especially chaps. 5, 9, and 10.)

The Gift of Prophecy

We need to have an accurate understanding of the gift of prophecy and a scriptural awareness that there are gifted leaders called prophets
(see chap. 6). The gift of prophecy refers to preaching, not fore-
telling the future. It means "to tell forth, to declare." The gift of
prophecy is not to be confused with the office of prophet. First
Corinthians 12:8, 10 defines the gift of prophecy: "For to one is given
the word of wisdom through the Spirit . . . to another prophecy."
God has not only given certain members of the Body of Christ the
gift of prophecy, but also given the church certain gifted leaders:
"God has appointed in the church, first apostles, second prophets,
third teachers" (v. 28). The prophet and the gift of prophecy are
thus distinct. The New Testament prophets belonged to a special
group (the first-century church) and a special time in history (the
apostolic era). They spoke after they had received the Word of God
directly. There are no prophets today, just as there are no Christ-
appointed apostles. That's because the written Word of God is complete, and there is no need today for special believers to convey God's
latest revelation.

Though the prophets have ceased, the gift of prophecy, or
preaching, still continues to confirm the Scripture already given.
That's why Paul says, "Pursue love, yet desire earnestly spiritual gifts,
but especially that you may prophesy" (14:1). The word "prophesy" means "preach." Preaching is defined by Paul's use of three words:
"But one who prophesies [preaches] speaks to men for edification
and exhortation and consolation" (v. 3). Preaching is building up,
encouraging, and comforting. Paul tells Timothy the best way to
preach: "Until I come, give attention to the public reading of
Scripture, to exhortation and teaching" (1 Tim. 4:13). Paul advo-
cates expository preaching as he says, in effect, "Read the text, explain
the text, apply the text." The implication is that much of the

preaching then, as in our day, was departing from the text.

Comparing the gift of prophecy with tongues, Paul says, "One who speaks in a tongue edifies himself; but one who prophesies edifies the church" (1 Cor. 14:4). Preaching was a dominant ministry, which took precedence over the gift of tongues.

There are some efforts today to play down the centrality of preaching, but preaching is still a gift of the Spirit. No worship service of the Body is complete without a declaration of God's truth. The preaching of the cross is still central in the gathering of the church. The standard of true preaching in the early church was whether or not the prophet's words squared with the words of Jesus Christ (1 Cor. 14:37). The gift of preaching today is exercised under the same standard—not the standard of a news magazine, or politics, or secular philosophy, or a book review, but the Word of God. Preaching (*kerygma*) always includes biblical doctrine (*didache*). The gift of preaching is therefore a Spirit-given and Spirit-energized ability to proclaim the truths of Jesus Christ to the Body.

The Gift of Teaching

There is a gift of teaching, and there is also a gifted leader, the teacher (1 Cor. 12:28). Teachers were recognized and appointed in the early church and given specific positions to teach, even as now. Some of the great professors in evangelical seminaries, and some of the great Bible teachers who travel the world, are recognized as divinely appointed teachers, given to the church.

While many believers may have the gift of teaching, some may not be appointed to a formal teaching office in the church. Basically, teaching is the ability to impart the truths of the Word of God. It's not the same as preaching. Proclaiming the gospel is one gift, but it is something else to sit down with a newborn babe and instruct him or her in the things of God. That is the gift of teaching. It can be exercised in a Sunday School class, in a home, or in a counseling situation. Of course, it's possible for a person to have a gift that includes both preaching and teaching.

While teaching is a special gift, every Christian is to some degree a teacher. All believers are responsible to teach fellow believers, their own families, or others who need the truth (Gal. 6:6; 2 Tim. 2:2, 15).

In the Body, preaching and teaching provide a balanced ministry of evangelism and edification. Preaching is motivating; teaching is instructing. They go side by side.

The Gift of Faith

Faith is another one of the Spirit-given gifts. All believers have faith, but some have a special gift of faith. I believe this could just as well be called "the gift of prayer." Believers with this gift receive an extra measure of faith and confidence that God will answer prayer—and that He will sometimes do so in extraordinary ways when all other resources have been exhausted.

The Gift of Wisdom

This is the ability to see deeply into the mysteries of God. It is the kind of insight that sees what the natural eye can't see; that hears what the natural ear cannot hear. It's the ability to take a phrase of Scripture, extract from it all of God's truth, and apply it to life. A simple definition of wisdom is "the application of spiritual truth." In a sense, all believers are to have wisdom (Col. 1:9; James 1:5). But some rise above the regular level to minister to the Body in a unique way.

The Gift of Knowledge

If wisdom is the application of truth, knowledge is the academic understanding of it. Those with the gift of knowledge are the scholars who do biblical, theological, linguistic, and archeological research. Some spend all their lives studying ancient manuscripts, ancient artifacts, and all kinds of scholarly problems. They are able, by the Spirit of God, to search out the facts. On their work we build our faith. The Bible in modern languages didn't simply drop out of heaven; it took years and years of study to determine which Hebrew, Aramaic, and Greek manuscripts were the most accurate for translation.

Because a person has a high IQ doesn't mean this person has the gift of knowledge (or the gift of wisdom). Moreover, some of the wisest people I have met didn't have an extraordinary IQ, but they had the Spirit-given gift of wisdom. Wisdom and knowledge are spiritual gifts, not intellectual; they are given by a sovereign act of the Holy Spirit. A believer's insights into Scripture, therefore, do not depend on our own intelligence.

All Christians are responsible to study to show themselves approved unto God. All believers should seek after wisdom and knowledge (1 Cor. 1:5, 30). And yet there is a sense in which some Christians are specially gifted and uniquely called to minister to the Body in those areas.

The Discernment of Spirits

Since God wanted to protect the church from false doctrine, He gave certain members the ability to determine which teacher was right and which was wrong. The Body faces continual opposition from a host of demons who pose as messengers of light, trying to counterfeit the gifts of the Spirit and sap the energy of the church. Because of this, God gave a certain gift, beyond natural insight, so that believers could discern between God and Satan.

Peter used this gift of discernment when he asked Ananias, "Why has Satan filled your heart to lie to the Holy Spirit?" (Acts 5:3) Under ordinary circumstances, another person would not have known that Ananias and his wife were lying about what they had received for their property, but God gave Peter the ability to discern the truth. Every Christian in a sense is to be discerning. "Beloved, do not believe every spirit, but test the spirits to see whether they are from God; because many false prophets have gone out into the world" (1 John 4:1).

The Gift of Showing Mercy

Next, we come to the love gifts. Though all the gifts are to be ministered in love, there are three distinct love gifts that minister to the Body. The first is the gift of showing mercy. Most Christians can't preach a sermon, but they can do deeds of loving-kindness. This is Christ's love, manifested by the Holy Spirit, through the believers to the Body. Such love is not just sympathy—it's not exercised out of duty. Rather, some Christians just have that spiritual gift of compassionate love that causes them to show kindness to others. Some of the greatest testimony to Christ is given without a word being spoken as we quietly express love to someone.

The Apostle James asked this convicting question: "If a brother or sister is without clothing and in need of daily food, and one of you says to them, 'Go in peace, be warmed and be filled'; and yet you do not give them what is necessary for their body; what use is that?" (James 2:15-16)

The implication is obvious. All Christians are to be merciful and kind; yet some have the gift of showing mercy to the whole Body. They set the example for the rest of us.

The Gift of Exhortation

The Greek word translated "exhortation" (Rom. 12:8) refers to one who comes along to help. Exhortation is not standing in the pulpit browbeating people. It is not necessarily even a public gift, though it may be used as such (1 Cor. 14:3). It is the ability to come alongside someone and encourage that person. Jesus said, "And I will ask the Father, and He will give you another Helper, that He may be with you forever" (John 14:16).

The Helper is the Holy Spirit. The Greek word translated "Helper" is *paracletos* (from which we get the name Paraclete), and it means "one called alongside." The believer with the gift of exhortation, in the power of the true Paraclete, is used to come alongside members of the Body to comfort, console, encourage, counsel, and exhort. This is the gift that qualifies some Christians to exercise an especially helpful and necessary personal ministry in the Body. Again, though there are some who are gifted in exhortation, all Christians are to put their arms around each other every day to comfort, counsel, and encourage. The writer to the Hebrews says, "Encourage one another day after day" (Heb. 3:13).

The Gift of Giving

This third love gift directly concerns the ministry of material goods, such as providing food, clothing, money, or shelter for those in need. This is related to the Holy Spirit's supervision of everything a Christian possesses. It doesn't relate at all to how much we have; some with the gift of giving are the poorest members of the Body. If those who have the gift of giving would release themselves and give in the energy of the Spirit, Christians could care for material needs in the church, and there would be no need for any believers to turn to government welfare.

Of course, the Bible commands that no Christian should miss the joy of regular giving to support the church: "Let each one do just as he has purposed in his heart; not grudgingly or under compulsion; for God loves a cheerful giver" (2 Cor. 9:7).

The Gift of Administration

The gift of administration belongs to those in places of spiritual authority. Pastors, teachers, or evangelists exercise it. Paul urges other believers to respect those who have these gifts: "But we request of you, brethren, that you appreciate those who diligently labor among you, and have charge over you in the Lord and give you instruction" (1 Thes. 5:12).

Christians who have been divinely placed over other believers are to care for them—not to lord it over them, or to hammer them down, or to brutally subject them. Those gifted in administration are to diligently teach and instruct others: "Let the elders who rule well be considered worthy of double honor, especially those who work hard at preaching and teaching" (1 Tim. 5:17; see also Heb. 13:7, 17, 24).

Of course, this gift is not limited to pastors in local churches. It is also exercised by those in leadership in mission societies, youth organizations, and evangelistic associations.

The Gift of Ministry or Helps

The terms *ministry* and *helps* both mean service; they are gifts of assistance. The early deacons exercised this gift (the Greek word translated "deacon" means "service"). Christians with this gift are helpers—persons who labor behind the scenes. This gift, like all the others, is to be evident to some degree in all Christians: "Through love serve one another" (Gal. 5:13). Yet some are especially grace-gifted for works of service to the Body.

In this chapter we have discussed eleven edifying gifts, or ones that build up. Every gift was characteristic of Jesus Christ during His earthly ministry. He was a teacher; He was full of faith; He was wisdom personified; He had all knowledge; He was the discerner of spirits;

He showed mercy; He was the true *paraclete;* He was the ultimate giver; He was ruler and leader; and He was servant and minister.

The church, a new Body formed by Christ, is to do what Christ's fleshly body did—manifest His nature. Since all these gifts were part of His fleshly body, all are also a part of His spiritual Body. Spiritual gifts are the reproduction of Christ's ministry. They are grace gifts (*charismata*) given to the church by the Holy Spirit so that it may be the continuing life of Christ.

The reason every Christian should share in all these ministries to some degree is that all believers are called to be like Jesus Christ. Everything that characterized Him should also be true, though imperfectly, of each member of His Body. If the Christian's testimony is to be totally effective, the world will have to see in us the reflection of Jesus Christ Himself. It is vitally important for all believers to know their spiritual gift and to use it. That way the Body's witness will be effective, and each member in a personal way will reflect all of Christ's attributes. The key is to allow the Holy Spirit to be in control as we use our gifts.

9

The Fellowship
of the Body

As a human body is formed by tissues, muscles, bones, ligaments, and organs that are designed to work together, the Body of Christ is composed of members who are responsible to one another. No member properly functions detached from the rest of the Body, just as a person's lungs can't be removed, placed in another room, and still be expected to keep the person breathing. The health of the Body, its witness, and its testimony are dependent on all members faithfully ministering to one another.

As believers in Christ, we are one in position. The Holy Spirit has placed all of us into the Body of Christ, and that same Spirit dwells within each believer (1 Cor. 12:13).

Though Christians are one in position, unfortunately they are not one in practice—in the daily grind of living and loving together. When Jesus prayed "that they may all be one" (John 17:21), He was praying for Christians to live as one.

This practical, experiential unity of the Body is manifest by service and fellowship. Service includes the individual spiritual gift of service (see the previous chapter), but in this chapter we are enlarging the concept to encompass the exercising of all the gifts within a context of genuine fellowship.

The New Testament word for fellowship is *koinonia*. It means communion or intimate communication. God designed His people for fellowship: "It is not good for the man to be alone" (Gen. 2:18). The church, the Body of Christ, should be the epitome of fellowship.

It was never intended to be only a building—a place where lonely people walk in, listen, and walk out still alone—but a place of fellowship. In his book *Dare to Live Now!* Bruce Larson says,

> The neighborhood bar is possibly the best counterfeit there is to the fellowship Christ wants to give His Church. It's an imitation, dispensing liquor instead of grace, escape rather than reality. But it is a permissive, accepting, and inclusive fellowship. It is unshockable, it is democratic. You can tell people secrets and they usually don't tell others, or want to.

> The bar flourishes not because most people are alcoholics, but because God has put into the human heart the desire to know and be known, to love, and be loved, and so many seek a counterfeit at the price of a few beers (Grand Rapids: Zondervan, 1965, 110).

The genius of the church is that it can meet this need for fellowship. But the need is not met simply by attending the Sunday services—whether they be in a small assembly where everyone is known or in a large congregation where many people remain anonymous. A desperate need for personal, intimate fellowship exists in the church today. And this fellowship, like the ministering of the gifts, is essential to practical unity. It is Body life!

The New Testament teaches four things about fellowship: its basis, its nature, what endangers it, and its responsibilities.

The Basis of Fellowship

There is much phony fellowship today—people get together on all kinds of pretenses. But the basis of Body fellowship is not the need of the surrounding community, or some common social or religious goal. The basis is found in the word *koinonia*, which suggests sharing and communion—a common ground. Believers have a common ground, a partnership with something to share.

"What we have seen and heard we proclaim to you also, that you also may have fellowship with us; and indeed our fellowship is with the Father, and with His Son Jesus Christ" (1 John 1:3). That is the ground of Christian fellowship.

John relates the gospel to what he personally experienced (v. 1). He tells of his relationship with Jesus Christ. He does that because the gospel is the basis of Christian fellowship. John is telling his readers, in effect, "I want you to know the same God and the same Christ I know, so that we may have common ground for fellowship."

The proclamation of the gospel is not an end in itself—it creates a fellowship of believers (Phil. 1:5). The beautiful, meaningful fellowship that Christ and His disciples enjoyed while He was on earth was not meant to be limited to them, but was intended to extend to all of us who are in the Body of Christ. In a sense, we are in the fellowship of the apostles (Eph. 3 and Heb. 2), but primarily our fellowship involves the Father, the Son, the Spirit, and every other believer in history (2 Cor. 13:14; Eph. 4:4-6; Phil. 2:1). Salvation made it happen.

God planned to bring believers into fellowship. "God is faithful, through whom you were called into fellowship with His Son, Jesus Christ our Lord" (1 Cor. 1:9). God is not some distant, cosmic deity. Through His sovereign grace He brought us into His fellowship, by faith in Jesus Christ. Paul speaks of "a common faith" (Titus 1:4), a single body of truth of which every Christian is a part.

Fellowship in this context becomes a specifically Christian word, referring to a common participation in eternal life that comes by the grace of God, the saving work of Christ, and is enhanced by the indwelling of the Holy Spirit. All preaching in the church is meant to create a human fellowship, rising spontaneously out of the divine fellowship.

Technically, no Christian is at any time out of fellowship with God since the relationship between the believer and God is permanent. When two people are married, for example, there are times when they won't speak to each other, and yet their partnership continues. Partners in business may not like each other, but they remain partners. Similarly, when a Christian is not behaving as a partner with God ought to (he or she may be violating some of the partnership standards), the partnership still continues. Paul refers to the "fellowship in the gospel," which continues "from the first day [salvation]" until the present (Phil. 1:5, KJV).

When we are blessed and feeling good about our relationship with the Lord, we often say, "I'm in fellowship." When we are not excited about the Lord, and there is sin in our life and indifference about our Christian walk, we say, "I'm out of fellowship." Strictly speaking, that is not true. We are always in fellowship, but we may not be experiencing the joy of it.

If you want to evaluate your Christian life correctly, say, "I'm experiencing complete joy in my fellowship with the Father," or, "I'm not experiencing the joy of my fellowship with God." The Apostle John says, "These things we write, so that our joy may be made complete" (1 John 1:4). That is the issue—the difference in the partnership when there is complete joy and when it is absent.

It is sin that affects the joy of our fellowship with God. That's why it is so important to remember 1 John 1:9: "If we confess our sins, He is faithful and righteous to forgive us our sins and to cleanse us from all unrighteousness." That kind of confession should become the pattern of life for us. It is not an ongoing confession to maintain our salvation, as if we are fearful of losing it. The kind of confession that acknowledges our need theologically to become right with God happened just once—when we were saved. John is speaking of the confession we will want to constantly maintain after we come into fellowship with God. We acknowledge our daily sin, ask forgiveness, receive it, and again enjoy complete fellowship with the Lord.

The Nature of Fellowship

The nature of fellowship is illustrated in several New Testament examples.

> And the congregation of those who believed were of one heart and soul; and not one of them claimed that anything belonging to him was his own; but all things were common property to them. . . .

> For there was not a needy person among them, for all who were owners of lands or houses would sell them and bring the proceeds of the sales, and lay them at the apostles' feet; and they would be distributed to each, as any had need (Acts 4:32, 34-35).

Those early believers in Jerusalem shared everything. That was true fellowship. It had a marked effect on the world, and as a result, many persons were brought to Christ:

> And all those who had believed were together, and had all things in common; and they began selling their property and possessions, and were sharing them with all, as anyone might have need. And day by day continuing with one mind in the temple, and breaking bread from house to house, they were taking their meals together with gladness and sincerity of heart, praising God, and having favor with all the people. And the Lord was adding to their number day by day those who were being saved (2:44-47).

That is the oneness Christ had prayed for. Because those outside the church could see this unity and love, they were more readily convinced of Jesus' identity.

Paul describes a later example of fellowship among churches: "For Macedonia and Achaia have been pleased to make a contribution for the poor among the saints in Jerusalem" (Rom. 15:26). The wealthier church in Europe collected money to send to poorer Christians in Jerusalem. In Christian fellowship believers desire to bear one another's burdens, share needs, and teach (Rom. 1:11-12; Gal. 6:2, 6). The early Christians enjoyed a genuine fellowship of money, food, homes, prayer, love, spiritual blessing, and teaching.

Paul himself needed this kind of fellowship. He didn't just ease through his ministries by himself. "But God, who comforts the depressed, comforted us by the coming of Titus" (2 Cor. 7:6). Paul also told Timothy, "Make every effort to come before winter" (2 Tim. 4:21). He cherished fellowship and looked forward to it.

What is Christian fellowship today? Is it going to the "fellowship hall" in the church basement, to a picnic, or a Sunday School class party? Is it a committee meeting? Fellowship occurs when Christians get together to discuss the Word of God and share concerns in the power of the Holy Spirit. There are times when getting together with Christians may seem a wasted effort, but when you experience true fellowship, you'll come away warmed in spirit.

When there is true fellowship, Christians don't judge one another. They don't bite and devour one another. They don't provoke, envy, lie to, speak evil of, or grumble about one another. Since true fellowship builds up, Christians receive one another and are kind and tenderhearted toward one another. They forbear and forgive one another, serve one another, practice hospitality ungrudgingly to one another, admonish, instruct, submit to, and comfort one another. That is the true fellowship of the Body. It is life touching life to bring blessing and spiritual growth.

The Danger to Fellowship

As we noted earlier, a believer's fellowship with God is never broken because it is an eternal partnership (John 10:28-29). But because God is holy, sin destroys the joy of the believer's fellowship.

If we sin willfully and continually, we have purposely broken trust with God and have willfully spurned His love. Sin doesn't change God's love, nor does it mean the one who sins doesn't love Him. It does mean that a sinning Christian can lose the joy of communion with God. Usually our prayer life goes, our Bible reading goes, and we drift away from relating to other Christians—all because we don't want to be confronted with God.

The symbol of Body fellowship is the Communion service. When Christians meet around the Lord's Table and partake of the cup and the bread, they are symbolizing Jesus' saving death, which is the basis of fellowship. The word *koinonia* in Greek conveys the concepts of fellowship and communion. Paul writes, "Is not the cup of blessing which we bless a sharing in the blood of Christ? Is not the bread which we break a sharing in the body of Christ? . . . You cannot drink the cup of the Lord, and the cup of demons; you cannot partake of the table of the Lord, and the table of demons" (1 Cor. 10:16, 21).

How could Christians drink of the cup of the Lord, celebrate their fellowship with Him, and then go out and fellowship with demons? That is blasphemous and makes a mockery of the cross. Sin is communion with Satan and his fallen angels. So Paul warns, "Let a man examine himself, and so let him eat of the bread and drink of the cup. For he who eats and drinks, eats and drinks judgment to himself, if he does not judge the body rightly" (11:28-29).

How did God judge believers in the Corinthian church who partook of Communion sinfully? "For this reason many among you are weak and sick, and a number sleep [die]" (v. 30). Their sin violated all that the cross stood for. In fact, their participation was a mockery serious enough to sometimes cause their own death. That's why Paul warns us not to go to the Lord's Table without examining ourselves to be sure we're not at the same time having fellowship with demons.

Sin also breaks the joy of a Christian's fellowship with other believers. It shatters the unity of the Body. Your sin affects me because it limits my fellowship, and it limits the use of your gifts on my behalf. A Christian can't say, "I can do what I want; it won't affect anyone else." Pride, lust, materialism, failure to minister one's gift, ceasing to pray, spiritual laziness, not yielding to the Holy Spirit—all these sins and others destroy fellowship within the Body.

When a believer acknowledges his or her sin and confesses it to God, that sin will not become a pattern. Therefore, it will not affect the fellowship of the Body the way continual, prolonged sin does. When I sin and immediately confess it and repent of it, I find the joy of my fellowship is unbroken. But when sin persists, the joy of fellowship is destroyed. The danger to fellowship, then, is sin without repentance.

The Responsibilities of Fellowship

We have a responsibility to maintain fellowship by doing specific deeds for other believers. These actions are the "one anothers" of the New Testament.

Confess Your Sins to One Another

James 5:16 contains this command: "Confess your sins to one another, and pray for one another." One way to maintain the fellowship of the Body of Christ is to confess our sins to other Christians.

Imagine what a depth of honesty, beauty, and understanding would be brought to Christian fellowship if believers could openly share their sins. They need to realize that when they share problems, their fellow Christians will often say, "That's amazing; I have the same problem." Believers could more intelligently pray for and minister to one another if they knew they struggled with the same problems as other members of the Body.

Too often, however, Christians put little glass bubbles around themselves and present themselves as "super saints," as if they don't have a problem in the world. They are not willing to share openly, to expose their sins and problems to a fellow believer. They don't know what it is to have someone else say, "That's the same thing I'm going through. You pray for me, and I'll pray for you." One time a brother in Christ confessed a sin to me and promised to tell me each time he committed it. Later, he told me that the promise prevented him from committing the sin again.

James said, "Confess your sins to one another." That may or may not be considered good psychological therapy, but spiritually it is a tremendous preventative to sin. At some point Christians need to break through their isolation, crucify their egos, and begin to share and confess their sins to one another. There is no priesthood in the Body except the priesthood of believers. Confession of sins is one believer confessing to *one* other—not publicly before the whole church or the world.

If a believer has wronged a fellow believer, the sinning believer should go to the one sinned against. Christ commands us, "If therefore you are presenting your offering at the altar, and there remember that your brother has something against you, leave your offering there before the altar, and go your way, first be reconciled to your brother, and then come and present your offering" (Matt. 5:23-24). You are not to pay homage to God until you have made everything right with other believers.

Confession of sin to one another results in a more pure fellowship of people who know and love one another and understand one another's needs, anxieties, temptations, and sins. Each Christian has this responsibility in the Body. What strength Christians would find in such a community!

Forgive One Another
Some Christians have a hard time forgiving one another, but all believers are commanded to forgive fellow believers. Nevertheless, you sometimes hear people in the Body say things such as, "Well, if some-

body ever did that to me, I'd never forgive him!" Such an attitude is unworthy of a Christian.

Paul told those in the church at Corinth, "Sufficient for such a one is this punishment" (2 Cor. 2:6). That means you should not hold sin over a fellow believer's head for the rest of his or her life. On the contrary, "You should rather forgive and comfort him, lest somehow such a one be overwhelmed by excessive sorrow. Wherefore I urge you to reaffirm your love for him" (vv. 7-8).

When Christians sin, they have enough problems with the consequences without other Christians holding the sin over them. The other Christians are to go to them and forgive them. We find this additional guidance in Paul's admonition to the Colossians: "Bearing with one another, and forgiving each other, whoever has a complaint against any one; just as the Lord forgave you, so also should you" (Col. 3:13). No one deserves to be forgiven by Christ. Therefore, it is not right to accept Christ's forgiveness and then refuse to extend forgiveness to a fellow Christian (Eph. 4:32).

Forgiveness balances confession. When another believer confesses his or her sin to you, you are to forgive. If someone confesses, "I just want you to know that for ten years I have hated you. I've been talking behind your back," the Christian reaction should be forgiveness. When there is that kind of mutual concern in the Body of Christ, our fellowship and unity is strengthened.

Bear One Another's Burdens

Galatians 6:2 exhorts us to "bear one another's burdens, and thus fulfill the law of Christ." Burden-bearing means sympathetically loving one another and holding one another accountable. But we can't bear another Christian's burden unless that person shares it. So burden-bearing happens only when it follows in the sequence of fellowship's responsibilities: believers confessing their sins, forgiving each other, and then carrying each other's burdens.

If we see a brother or sister who is sinning, we have a spiritual obligation to tell him or her so—in love (see Matt. 18:15). Paul says, even in reference to an elder, "Those [elders] who continue in sin, rebuke in the presence of all, so that the rest also may be fearful of sinning" (1 Tim. 5:20).

The responsibility to confront a professing Christian about his or her sin also belongs to the entire local assembly, not just individual believers. The church might even need to put a person out of the fellowship (Matt. 18:17; 1 Cor. 5:5), if he or she continues in sin. Paul told the Corinthians "to deliver such a one to Satan" (v. 5). Paul told Timothy that he was delivering Hymenaeus and Alexander to Satan, that they might be taught not to blaspheme (1 Tim. 1:20). We usually think the sinning believer needs to be in church, but the Bible says to put that person out because sin destroys the purity of the fellowship. Jesus gives the pattern for such dismissal in Matthew 18:15-17. A believer continuing in sin must be brought to the place of repentance before God. In the early church, sinning brothers and sisters were put out in two ways: They were eliminated from the Lord's Table, and they were put out of the fellowship of other believers. They were still regarded as Christians, but they were removed lest they taint the fellowship and in the hope that removal would bring them to repentance.

Imagine what would happen if every church, through its elders, called a person to come before the congregation and said, "Now, we want to report what you did." If our fellowship in the Body were truly working, scenes like that would not be viewed as strange. They would occur as often as necessary and would have a purifying effect on us all. However, most Christians are afraid to exercise this responsibility. If they discover someone else's sin, they either keep it to themselves or gossip about it.

The point of being accountable to one another about sins is not only to restrict sin within the Body, but also to get Christians to open up and be honest with one another. As we have emphasized throughout this book, the church is a fellowship where every member is to be a minister. We need to be ready to rebuke sin in one another. Paul said to Titus in regard to certain Christians in Crete: "For this cause reprove them severely that they may be sound in the faith" (Titus 1:13). If we find someone teaching false doctrine, we are to tell that person so. Paul further admonished Titus: "These things speak and exhort and reprove with all authority. Let no one disregard you" (2:15).

Once we have rebuked a brother or sister about a sin, and they truly repent, it is time to restore them: "Brethren, even if a man is caught in any trespass, you who are spiritual, restore such a one in a spirit of gentleness; looking to yourself, lest you too be tempted" (Gal. 6:1). Pick them up and say, "Now let me show you what the Word of God says about this. Let's pray together—let's get back on the right track." That is restoring and caring in love. We haven't done our duty if we stop with rebuke.

We are also to take special care of the weaker brother or sister—not to offend him or her. We are not to abuse our Christian liberty and cause offense (Rom. 14:13, 19).

Love One Another

Loving equally with no favoritism is one of Paul's important themes (Rom. 12:10, 16; 13:8; 15:5, 7), and it is the central thrust of Christian fellowship. The fellowship of the Body is shattered when we show preference. Showing no favoritism means esteeming all above ourselves. John said, "Beloved, let us love one another" (1 John 4:7).

Peter also called for this when he wrote, "Fervently love one another from the heart" (1 Peter 1:22). "Fervently" is a word from the medical vocabulary that means "stretched." Christians are to stretch their love like an extended muscle that reaches out to all. First Peter further defines this kind of equal, stretched love as "sympathetic" (3:8), "hospitable to one another" (4:9), submissive (5:5), and physically demonstrative (v. 14).

Paul says this kind of love should include caring service for one another (Gal. 5:13); patience and forbearance (Eph. 4:2; Col. 3:13); and result in kindness, tenderheartedness, and forgiveness (Eph. 4:32; Col. 3:13).

Encourage One Another

Paul, writing to the discouraged Thessalonian believers, encouraged them to "comfort one another" (1 Thes. 4:18; 5:11). Twice in Hebrews we read "encourage one another" (3:13; 10:25). "Comfort" and "encourage" come from the same Greek word, *parakaleō*, which means "to come alongside to help." This is the ministry of personal care. In the New Testament, *parakaleō* is often used in reference to the brevity of time. In 1 Thessalonians, it is in the context of the Rapture; in Hebrews, of coming judgment. It carries the idea of urgency. Christians are to help one another in view of the return of Jesus (Rev. 22:12).

Build Up One Another

Three additional "one anothers" make a fitting conclusion for this chapter. The first one is to "build up one another" (Rom. 14:19; 1 Thes. 5:11). The tool for this is the Word of God. Paul commended the Ephesian elders "to God and to the word of His grace, which is able to build you up" (Acts 20:32). Christians have a far-reaching responsibility to know the Word, not only for their own sakes, but also for edifying one another. Personal ignorance of Scripture brings damage to the entire Body.

Admonish One Another

The second is "to admonish one another" (Rom. 15:14; Col. 3:16). Apparently, this kind of encouraging counsel implies sin is present. It means encouraging a brother or sister in sin to turn from it and live righteously and godly. Admonishing is never harsh, unloving, or abusive. It is to be done gently (2 Thes. 3:14-15).

Pray for One Another

The third "one another" is "pray for one another" (James 5:16). This responsibility is at the heart of relationships in the Body. It is something no Christian can avoid and still be a contributing member of the Body. Such mutual prayer is based on the honest sharing of personal needs and the personal discipline involved in setting aside a regular time for it.

In summary, fellowship in the Body results in joy. Christ came "that your joy may be made full" (John 16:24)—joy resulting from pure fellowship with God and with one another. Such fellowship is possible; God planned it that way. It is each Christian's responsibility to make fellowship in the Body all that God intends it to be.

10

The Witness of the Body

From the beginning God has desired to communicate with humanity, to manifest His truth. His crowning act of communication was sending Jesus Christ into the world. After His death and resurrection, Christ ascended into heaven and is no longer visible on earth. But God, through Christ, sent the Holy Spirit to manifest Himself in another Body—the Body of Christ, the church. This time it was not one body physically, but many bodies, making up one spiritual Body. Christ is in the Body, manifesting His glory and all His attributes, just as He did in His human body when He was here for thirty-three years. When Christ's physical body was here, He manifested love, holiness, wisdom, power, and all the authority of God. Christians, as members of the Body of Christ, are to reflect these attributes to the world.

God's will for this earthly Body is that all members "attain to the unity of the faith, and of the knowledge of the Son of God . . . to the measure of the stature which belongs to the fulness of Christ" (Eph. 4:13).

We read that God has predestined believers to be conformed into the image of His Son (Rom. 8:28-29). Grasp the miraculous nature of this statement. Christ can take our human bodies, subject to sin and death, physically frail, and make them into His temple—literally dwelling in them and planting in them His glory so that we might manifest Him to the world. What a miracle! What a demonstration of God's power in love!

Every member of the Body, therefore, can and should be a witness. "You shall receive power," said Jesus, "when the Holy Spirit has come upon you; and you shall be My witnesses" (Acts 1:8). There is no waiver given nor excuse accepted. "Therefore if any man is in Christ, he is a new creature; the old things passed away; behold, new things have come. Now all these things are from God, who reconciled us to Himself through Christ, and gave us the ministry of reconciliation" (2 Cor. 5:17-18). Anyone reconciled to Christ has the ministry of telling others about Him. In the same chapter the Apostle Paul asserts, "Therefore, we are ambassadors for Christ, as though God were entreating through us; we beg you on behalf of Christ, be reconciled to God" (v. 20).

In the midst of these and related commands from Scripture, it is crucial to remember that the Holy Spirit empowers us—individually and as a Body—to witness: "When the Helper comes, whom I will send to you from the Father, that is the Spirit of truth, who proceeds from the Father, He will bear witness of Me, and you will bear witness also, because you have been with Me from the beginning" (John 15:26-27).

On Trial

In those two verses we discover the basic concept of the Body's witness. The word "witness" takes us into a law court. We see a judge on the bench and a prisoner on trial. We hear the case argued by the prosecution, then by the defense. Both call witnesses to substantiate their arguments. The setting implies that Christians, as individual members of the Body, are witnesses in a trial, so to speak. Jesus Christ is on trial. The judge is the world. The defense attorney is the Holy Spirit. The prosecutor is Satan with his lies and accusations. Christians are witnesses.

Jesus Christ is on trial before the world—not before the Sanhedrin, not before Pilate, not before Herod Antipas, but before the bar of world opinion. The world judges Christ based on witnesses. Some people judge Him to be a fake; some, a good man; others, a moral teacher; still others, a liar; and so on. If a witness tears down the claims of Jesus Christ by the kind of life he or she lives, it would be better if that person were out of the courtroom altogether. That witness only confuses the issue. As we saw in chapter 8, the word "Helper" is *paracletos*, "one called alongside for defense." The Holy Spirit defends Christ. He calls members of the Body to witness and confirm the testimony of Christ (John 15: 27). All Christians are witnesses, either helping or hindering the cause of Christ.

The Body witnesses by its unity (13:34-35; 17:7). Can you imagine the impact that a united church would have on this world? I don't mean an ecumenical church in which all members ignore or minimize doctrine, throw their arms around each other, and march off to battle over the latest social issue. The true Body of Christ needs to be one. Sadly, it is not. Today the Body's testimony to unity is pathetically weak. The church's witness too often is composed of negative elements: strife, division, carnality, and confusion.

God's Word, however, sets forth six positive aspects of the Body's witness: to the world, of the Son, by the Father, through the Holy Spirit, in the individual member, and in the total Body.

Witness Is to the World

Christians will not understand the nature of their witness until they understand what the world is. Jesus spoke about its characteristics. Generated and controlled by Satan, "the world" is the entire system of evil that operates on the earth through demons and people who don't know God (John 8:44). The prince and ruler of this world is therefore the devil. True, the world is passing away (1 John 2:17), but while it lasts, it is the absolute antagonist of the church. Indeed, the world's hatred of the church is deep and bitter.

The following verses about the Body's witness to the world are in a context of the world's hostility and hatred toward believers:

> If the world hates you, you know that it has hated Me before it hated you. If you were of the world, the world would love its own; but because you are not of the world, but I chose you out of the world, therefore the world hates you. . . . But all these things they will do to you for My name's sake, because they do not know the One who sent Me. . . . If I had not done among them the works which no one else did, they would not have sin; but now they have both seen and hated Me and My Father

as well. But they have done this in order that the word may be fulfilled that is written in their Law, "They hated Me without a cause." . . . These things I have spoken to you, that you may be kept from stumbling. They will make you outcasts from the synagogue; but an hour is coming for everyone who kills you to think that he is offering service to God. And these things they will do, because they have not known the Father, or Me (John 15:18-19, 21, 24-25; 16:1-3).

The world hates Christians. It ostracizes them and kills them. The world is also antagonistic to the gospel. But Jesus says believers must witness to such hostility: "When the Helper comes," you will confront the world and witness to it.

How is a member of the Body to react when he or she is faced with the opposition of the world? Should we retaliate in anger or withdraw in self-pity to our Bible study group? No! We are supposed to bear witness before the world whatever the cost—and count it all joy to suffer in Jesus Christ's place (Col. 1:24).

Witness Is of the Son

Jesus declared, "You will bear witness also, because you have been with Me" (John 15:27). Christ is on trial, and Christian testimony must be of Him.

Preaching centers on Jesus Christ throughout the New Testament. The Apostle John says of himself, "Who bore witness to the word of God and to the testimony of Jesus Christ" (Rev. 1:2). Later in the Book of Revelation he reiterates the idea of testifying to Christ: "And the dragon was enraged with the woman, and went off to make war with the rest of her offspring, who keep the commandments of God and hold to the testimony of Jesus" (12:17). Testimony was always directly associated with Jesus Christ. In fact, we also read that the Old Testament witnessed to Him: "For the testimony of Jesus is the spirit of prophecy" (19:10).

The apostles had no doubts that they were to witness to the Son. Jesus told them, "You shall be My witnesses" (Acts 1:8). Their sermons in the early church were always about Him. For instance, Peter preached to Cornelius and said,

You know of Jesus of Nazareth, how God anointed Him with the Holy Spirit and with power, and how He went about doing good, and healing all who were oppressed by the devil; for God was with Him. And we are witnesses of all the things He did both in the land of the Jews and in Jerusalem. And they also put Him to death by hanging Him on a cross. God raised Him up on the third day, and granted that He should become visible (10:38-40).

Much so-called witnessing has nothing to do with Jesus Christ. It talks about religion, or the church, or vaguely about God.

We say, "I witnessed to my friend."

"What did you say?"

"Well, I kind of let him know that I go to church."

Often our witnessing is only an autobiography, and we never get around to speaking of Christ. A Christian can give his or her entire "testimony" and the listener might know nothing more about Jesus than when the Christian started. Biblical witnessing is a testimony to Jesus Christ! It is proclaiming the great truths of His virgin birth, sinless life, atoning death, physical resurrection, ascension, and coming again.

Witness Is by the Father

When Jesus Christ sent the Holy Spirit, He really sent God's witness to this world: "When the Helper comes, whom I will send to you from the Father, that is the Spirit of truth, who proceeds from the Father, He will bear witness of Me" (John 15:26). It was the Father's supreme concern to bring honor and glory to the Son, and the Spirit helped Him. Jesus answered the Jews' question about His identity by saying, "If I glorify Myself, My glory is nothing; it is My Father who glorifies Me" (8:54).

Jesus said, in effect, "The Father is My chief witness. He is the one primarily concerned with communicating who I am. The Spirit who proceeds from the Father is sent to carry the Father's witness and plant it within you!"

The Father bore witness to the Son first through the Old Testament. "You search the Scriptures," Jesus said to the Jews, "because you think that in them you have eternal life; and it is these that bear witness of Me" (5:39). Jesus revealed additional things about the Old Testament witness to Himself as He spoke to the two disciples on the road to Emmaus: "And beginning with Moses and with all the prophets, He explained to them the things concerning Himself in all the Scriptures" (Luke 24:27).

The second way God witnessed to His Son was through Christ's works: "Jesus answered them, 'I told you, and you do not believe; the works that I do in My Father's name, these bear witness of Me'" (John 10:25). The miracles Jesus performed were the Father's witness. They revealed that Jesus is who He claimed to be. Later in John's Gospel, Jesus reasoned, "Do you not believe that I am in the Father, and the Father is in Me? The words that I say to you I do not speak on My own initiative, but the Father abiding in Me does His works" (14:10).

The third means of the Father's witness was through direct communication. God actually said in an audible voice, "This is My beloved Son" (Matt. 17:5). The Father, then, is the source of all witness about Christ, as recorded in Scripture: the Old Testament prophecies, the works Jesus did, the words He spoke, and the direct statements of the Father. Our Christian witness should be an echo of the Father's witness, and that will happen if we study the Word diligently and share it with others.

Witness Is through the Spirit

"When the Helper comes, whom I will send to you from the Father, that is the Spirit of Truth, who proceeds from the Father, He will bear witness of Me" (John 15:26). Whatever witness God the Father has in the world, He has through the Holy Spirit. The Spirit calls believers into court to testify. Since He is also "the Spirit of truth," this reveals the kind of testimony He gives. He cannot be a false witness; He is truth and always declares truth. If Jesus Himself ministered in the power of the Spirit, members of His Body must rely on the Holy Spirit's power to witness.

Today the Holy Spirit dwells within all believers. They are the vehicles carrying the witness that proceeds from the Father by the

Spirit. The Holy Spirit has no physical voice. His witnessing is through individual members of the Body. When Jesus promised to send the Spirit, He said, "He abides with you, and will be in you" (14:17). Acts 4:31 describes how witnessing through the Spirit occurred in the early church: "They [believers] were all filled with the Holy Spirit, and began to speak the word of God with boldness." Witnessing, then, is carrying the testimony of the Father and the Son, brought to us through the Spirit, and communicating it to the world.

Christians are qualified to witness not only because of the resident Holy Spirit, but also because they have experienced Jesus Christ firsthand. Christ's words were directed to the disciples gathered with Him in the Upper Room (John 15), but they also apply to believers today. We can be witnesses only if we experience what we are testifying about. To witness in a court case we must have been personally involved; secondhand testimony is unacceptable.

I will never forget the time I had to go to court to testify about a crime I'd seen. The court asked me three things: "What did you see?" "What did you hear?" "What did you feel?" I could address these questions because I was an eyewitness. The Apostle John places this truth about firsthand experience into the context of the Christian life: "What we have heard, what we have seen with our eyes . . . and our hands handled, concerning the Word of life . . . we proclaim to you also" (1 John 1:1, 3). Body witness is not a detached lecture about Jesus. Instead, it declares in a relevant way, "I have seen and heard the Christ, and He has touched my life."

Down through the ages this kind of character witness has been more precious than life itself. The Greek word *martus*, which means "witness," is the source of the term *martyr*. We identify that word with one who dies for his or her witness. Many times when the early believers stood up as witnesses for Christ, it cost them their lives. The Body of Christ needs more who will witness effectively, whatever the cost to their egos or their lives.

Witness Is in the Body

If the Holy Spirit indwells every individual member of the church, then logically He indwells the entire Body.

> For He Himself is our peace, who made both groups into one [Jew and Gentile], and broke down the barrier of the dividing wall, by abolishing in His flesh the enmity [that is, the antagonism between Jew and Gentile], which is the Law of commandments contained in ordinances, that in Himself He might make the two into one new man. . . . for through Him we both have our access in one Spirit to the Father. . . . in whom the whole building, being fitted together is growing into a holy temple in the Lord; in whom you [plural] also are being built together into a dwelling of God in the Spirit (Eph. 2:14-15, 18, 21-22).

The entire church, the Body of Christ, is the temple of the Holy Spirit, just as the individual member is. The Spirit indwells the Body to witness to the world of the Father and the Son.

The Body presents a single, collective testimony in two ways. First, the Body witnesses by its visible unity. Jesus prayed, "I do not ask in behalf of these [disciples] alone, but for those also who believe in Me through their word; that they may all be one; even as Thou, Father, art in Me, and I in Thee, that they also may be in Us; that the world may believe that Thou didst send Me" (John 17:20-21).

Today this Body witness is not from a unified Body. We are fragmented, each group trying to protect its own ideas. We haven't begun to see what God can do through a united testimony of Jesus from within the church. What an impact we would make if only the world could see us as one!

The second way the Body witnesses is by love. Jesus told the disciples that love is the mark of all genuine believers: "Little children, I am with you a little while longer. You shall seek Me; and as I said to the Jews, 'Where I am going, you cannot come,' now I say to you also. A new commandment I give to you, that you love one another, even as I have loved you, that you also love one another. By this all men will know that you are My disciples, if you have love for one another" (13:33-35). Christians would have a more powerful effect on this world if they consistently showed love for one another.

Individual members of the Body are the last link in the witness of the Father. The testimony started with the Father, about the Son, through the Spirit, and came to us. The testimony of Christ must not break down at our level. Each Christian, as a member of Christ's church, must do his or her part to witness. Each one of us must help create unity by ministering our spiritual gift, by loving, and by fulfilling the demands of fellowship. Then the mission of the Father in sending the Son will come to pass as God intended. God's blueprint for the Body is clear. But all the plans are useless, unfulfilled, unless you and I make them part of our lives. There is a world to be won; it will be won, as we are one!

Part of a Masterpiece

Commitment involves a personal vow by us to exercise the priorities God has mandated for the building of Christ's Body. We must be willing to aggressively dedicate ourselves to answer the prayer of our Lord for unity. We must realize we are a strategic part of a great masterpiece.

There is a famous story from the days when Sir Christopher Wren was building St. Paul's Cathedral in London. Wren was taking a tour one day and asked one of the building workers, "What are you doing?"

The workman replied, "I am cutting this stone to the right size."

He asked a second man working elsewhere, "What are you doing?"

"I am earning money," he retorted.

When Wren asked a third man, the man paused from his work and excitedly replied, "I am helping Sir Christopher Wren to build St. Paul's Cathedral!"

As Christians, we must remember our lofty position in the Body—we are here, in the Spirit's energy, working to help the Lord Jesus Christ build His church.

Since the principles are revealed only in the Word of God, diligent and systematic study is essential, not only for initial information and inspiration, but also for review, that we may be constantly remembering the priorities we have studied.

These truths about the proper functioning of Christ's Body must be taught from the pulpit, in Sunday School and Bible studies, through personal discipling, and family devotions. The church has allowed the divine principles we have considered in this book to lie dormant for too long.

It is most reassuring to realize that the whole plan for the church depends on a sovereign God for its accomplishment. But it is also sobering to recognize that the plan's implementation is also affected by our faithfulness in discipleship, careful study, and communication.

Finally, brethren, rejoice, be made complete, be comforted, be like-minded, live in peace; and the God of love and peace shall be with you. Greet one another with a holy kiss. All the saints greet you. The grace of the Lord Jesus Christ, and the love of God, and the fellowship of the Holy Spirit, be with you all (2 Cor. 13:11-14).

Personal and Group Study Guide

For Personal Study

Settle into your favorite chair with your Bible, a pen or pencil, and this book. Read a chapter, marking portions that seem significant to you. Write in the margins. Note where you agree, disagree, or question the author. Look at the relevant Scripture passages. Then turn to the questions listed in this study guide. If you want to trace your progress with a written record, use a notebook to record your answers, thoughts, feelings, and further questions. Refer to the text and to the Scriptures as you allow the questions to enlarge your thinking. And *pray*. Ask God to give you a discerning mind for truth, an active concern for others, and a greater love for Himself.

For Group Study

Plan ahead. Before meeting with your group, read and mark the chapter as if you were preparing for personal study. Glance through the questions making mental notes of how you might contribute to your group's discussion. Bring a Bible and the text to your meeting.

Arrange an environment that promotes discussion. Comfortable chairs arranged in a casual circle invite people to talk with each other. Then say, "We are here to listen and respond to each other—and to learn together." If you are the leader, simply be sure to sit where you can have eye contact with each person.

Promptness counts. Time is as valuable to many people as money. If the group runs late (because of a late start), these people will feel as robbed as if you had picked their pockets. So, unless you have a mutual agreement, begin and end on time.

Involve everyone. Group learning works best if everyone participates more or less equally. If you are a natural *talker*, pause before you enter the conversation. Then ask a quiet person what he or she thinks. If you are a natural *listener*, don't hesitate to jump into the discussion. Others will benefit from your thoughts—but only if you speak them. If you are the *leader*, be careful not to dominate the session. Of course, you will have thought about the study ahead of time, but don't assume that people are present just to hear you—as flattering as that may feel. Instead, help group members to make their own discoveries. Ask the questions, but insert your own ideas only as they are needed to fill gaps.

Pace the study. The questions for each session are designed to last about one hour. Early questions form the framework for later discussion, so don't rush by so quickly that you miss a valuable foundation. Later questions, however, often speak of the here and now. So don't dawdle so long at the beginning that you leave no time to "get personal." While the leader must take responsibility for timing the flow of questions, it is the job of each person in the group to assist in keeping the study moving at an even pace.

Pray for each other—together, or alone. Then watch God's hand at work in all of your lives.

Notice that each session includes the following features:

Session Topic—a brief statement summarizing the session.

Community Builder—an activity to get acquainted with the session topic and/or with each other.

Questions—a list of questions to encourage individual or group discovery and application.

Prayer Focus—suggestions for turning one's learning into prayer.

Optional Activities—supplemental ideas that will enhance the study.

Assignment—activities or preparations to complete prior to the next session.

1
The Formation of the Body

Session Topic
In love, God chose believers before the foundation of the world to be members of His Body, the church, that they should be holy, enjoy all His blessings, and share Christ with the world.

Community Builder *(Choose One)*
1. At one time or another, we've all applied for a job for which another applicant was eventually chosen. Were you especially disappointed after one of those occurrences? Did you consider the decision unfair? Why?
2. Worldly organizations are not formed the way the church is. What are some of the major differences in how man-made groups form, as compared to how Christ's Body was formed? What primary motivations, in your view, lead people to join worldly clubs, associations, etc.?

Group Discovery Questions
1. What was the mystery revealed to Paul in Ephesians 1?
2. What was the basis for God's choosing us? How did Paul respond when he realized this fact? Do you share the same joy? If not, would you like to?
3. Is the doctrine of God's election limited to Ephesians 1? Name at least three other references in which this truth is found.
4. If God's sovereignty is one side of the coin of divine election, what is the other side? (Rom. 10:9-11)
5. What prerequisites must Christians meet if they want to have fellowship with God? (Eph. 5:25-27)
6. What man-made legal custom is a good parallel to the results of divine election?
7. What is "the theme that runs throughout the Bible" and "the reason for everything God does"?

Prayer Focus
*Thank God for the love He showed you in choosing you to be a part of Christ's Body.
*A full understanding of how God's sovereignty and man's responsibility work together is difficult to have. Ask God to help you have a better grasp on this area of Scripture truth.

Optional Activities
1. Read Ephesians 1:3-14 and spend some extra time meditating on its truths. Read the passage in several good translations and identify as many basic Christian doctrines as you can.
2. Read all or a portion of John Murray's book *Redemption Accomplished and Applied* (Grand Rapids: Eerdmans, 1955). Part 2 is especially helpful in explaining what happens when we become a member of the Body.

Assignment
1. Memorize John 1:12-13.
2. Read chapter 2 of *The Body Dynamic*.

2
Know Your Position in the Body

Session Topic
All believers need to understand their position in the Body of Christ and then use the resources God provides to live out that position.

Community Builder *(Choose One)*
1. Have you ever had a job or been on a sports team in which you were uncertain about your role? How did it affect your performance? What was your biggest frustration in that situation?
2. How well did you understand your position in Christ before you read this chapter? How is a right perspective of our position in the Body different from today's popular concept of self-esteem? Discuss.

Group Discovery Questions
1. What kind of position does God impute to a person when he is saved?
2. How does growth and maturity, or lack of these, affect the believer's position in Christ? Cite a New Testament verse and an Old Testament one to support your answer.
3. What recurring pattern of teaching does Paul use in the first three chapters of Ephesians?
4. What does Paul mean when he uses the term "spirit" in Ephesians 1:17? What contemporary synonym might be appropriate for this idea?
5. It is essential for Christians to seek "wisdom and revelation." What two different aspects of knowledge was Paul referring to when he used this phrase? How important is individual IQ in this quest for understanding?
6. What does "the hope of His calling" include? (Eph. 1:18) What time span is involved with it?
7. What is the primary tool believers have for appreciating "the

riches of the glory of His inheritance"? Is it possible to define these riches precisely? Are they fully fathomable?

8. How should we understand God's power in relation to us? What object or substance is His power often compared to? What other significant things in the history of God's plan have resulted from this power?

9. What was the Apostle Paul's main instruction to Timothy when Timothy struggled and faced difficulty in his Christian life? What other counsel could Paul have conveyed to Timothy as a remedy for trials?

10. How many positional truths with corresponding practices are given in the list at the end of chapter 2? What does that suggest about the richness of salvation?

Prayer Focus
*Thank the Lord for all the guidance and instruction He has given you concerning your position in the Body.

*Think of a new Christian you know, or of one who has been a Christian longer but is struggling, and ask God to help that person know more fully the power he has available as a member of the Body of Christ.

Optional Activities
1. Over the next several weeks read and study Colossians 3:1-17. Meditate on the individual verses as you work through the passage. Record your thoughts on how this passage relates to knowing and practicing your position in the Body. Do a word study on some of the key words.

2. Spend extra time in the upcoming months working your way through the list in the "Position/Practice" table section at the end of this chapter. Try to look up all the verses in the list. Write out some of the most helpful ones on index cards and keep them in key spots around the home or office as reminders.

Assignment
1. Memorize 1 Thessalonians 5:24 and recite it to someone before your next meeting.

2. Read chapter 3 of *The Body Dynamic*.

3
Salvation: Entrance to the Body

Session Topic
Salvation through faith in Jesus Christ, which results in a new life of good works, is the only way we can enter the Body of Christ.

Community Builder *(Choose One)*
1. We have all heard many faulty views of what a Christian is. Unbelievers also express a variety of excuses for not embracing the biblical way to salvation. Share one of the more interesting or unusual excuses someone has given you.
2. Maps and traffic signs can help us find our way on streets and highways. What can happen if we don't follow our road map, or if we ignore a highway sign? Have such "oversights" ever produced bad consequences for you?

Group Discovery Questions
1. What is the natural man's basic problem?
2. What must happen to all truly saved people? What kind of changed lifestyle will result?
3. How does the average unbeliever have an inaccurate concept of sin and what constitutes being "a sinner"? Explain and illustrate your answer.
4. Can non-Christians ever perform good deeds? Are their motives necessarily always bad? Do such actions equal good works in the scriptural sense?
5. What is the main philosophy promoted by the world's system? Define this school of thought in one sentence.
6. To what does the word "desires" in Ephesians 2:3 refer? What are the sinful outworkings of such desire, as listed by Paul in Galatians 5:19-21?
7. What are two facets of God's love? What role does each play in our salvation?
8. What is God's ultimate purpose for us in salvation? How long does this purpose last and how secure is it?

9. What is absolutely essential about spiritual birth and life? (John 3:3-8) How can this be illustrated by what happens immediately after natural birth?

10. What is the proper sequence and place of good works in the Christian life? (Eph. 2:10)

Prayer Focus

*Ask the Lord to give you a greater motivation for doing good works. Pray that He would provide good opportunities for such works.

*Pray for the same unsaved friend or relative each day next week. Ask God that the person would turn from sin and the world's system to spiritual life and good works as a new member of the Body.

Optional Activities

1. Read a basic book on the nature of salvation and the new life in Christ. Two possibilities for your reading are: Charles Spurgeon's 1894 classic *All of Grace* (Chicago: Moody Press), or John Stott's book *Men Made New* (Downers Grove, Ill.: InterVarsity, 1966). Take notes on the book and look for an opportunity to share what you've learned with someone else.

2. Read John 10:1-30. Summarize in your own words the theme of the passage. How does this passage parallel our chapter's topic of entrance to the Body?

Assignment

1. Memorize 1 John 3:2.

2. Read chapter 4 of *The Body Dynamic.*

4
Releasing Power in the Body

Session Topic
Genuine spiritual power is released in the Body as each member becomes indwelt and strengthened by the Father, Son, and Holy Spirit.

Community Builder *(Choose One)*
1. Have you ever taken a motivational or self-help course in relation to your job or profession? Was it useful? How consistent were you in following through on the course's recommendations? Have several people in the group share experiences.
2. What part of your week are you most likely to feel your inner strength failing? What remedy do you first turn to when you need an energy boost? Would you recommend such a strategy to others? Why?

Group Discovery Questions
1. When God gives us things, how does He always do it? (Eph. 1:7; Phil. 4:19)
2. What happens when the believer's inner man is weak?
3. What are a couple of vital, practical elements in living the Spirit-filled life? Do you think Christians often make the process too complicated? Why and how?
4. What must take place in a believer's heart before Christ can feel at home and "settle down."
5. Besides Christ's death, what did the cross symbolize for first-century Christians? Describe in specifics how the symbolism worked.
6. When a believer has the fullness of God, he receives a measure of what in return? What will the believer then radiate to the world?
7. What is the ultimate goal of spiritual development or maturity in the Christian's life?

Prayer Focus
*Spend some extra time in prayer today and other days this week examining your heart, confessing sin, and making Christ the cen-

ter of your heart's thoughts and activities.

*If you know of another member of your church or someone else in your study group who is especially discouraged or weighed down by pressures and burdens, pray for that person. Later ask him how things are going.

Optional Activities

1. Read back through and meditate on Ephesians 3:14-21. Divide this prayer of Paul into the five aspects we analyzed here in chapter 4. Make a small prayer notebook just for this exercise and record your thoughts, questions, prayer requests, etc., regarding the five aspects of spiritual power. Monitor your future progress.

2. If you don't already have one, obtain a copy of *My Heart Christ's Home* and read it. Go through it enough times so that you become thoroughly familiar with its contents—so much so that you can easily share the outline with others.

Assignment

1. Using a different Bible translation from what you normally read and study in, memorize 2 Corinthians 4:7.

2. Read chapter 5 of *The Body Dynamic*.

5
Acting Like a Member in the Body

Session Topic
If a Christian knows the truth and understands his position in the Body, then he will have a godly lifestyle, characterized by the worthy walk of Ephesians 4:2-3.

Community Builder *(Choose One)*
1. How strictly do you think a private club, organization, or association should try to enforce its rules and standards? Should such groups even have formal guidelines of conduct? Have you ever joined an organization and then, after you learned of its specific expectations, wished you hadn't?
2. Can you think of a favorite teacher, pastor, or boss who was especially faithful in living out what he/she professed? Tell the group briefly why that integrity was such an example for you.

Group Discovery Questions
1. What can happen when duty is taught without corresponding doctrinal teaching?
2. What was the Apostle Paul's overall attitude concerning his imprisonment at Rome? How did such an attitude relate to his appeal that Christians walk worthy?
3. What can a godly life reveal to unbelievers? What might such a revelation produce in their lives?
4. What necessary characteristic of the worthy walk was basically a new concept to the first-century Greek world? Why do you think the Greeks (and Romans) had not appreciated that aspect of personal conduct before?
5. What is another translation for "gentleness" in the New Testament? Is that translation a better way to convey the word's meaning? Why or why not?
6. What would be the best way for you to react to a petty offense that someone hurls at you in a local church meeting? How would Jesus respond in the same situation?

7. What is the key to obtaining unity in the Body?

8. Who and what was the sign of spiritual authenticity in the Book of Acts?

9. In addition to the kind of response that is part of salvation, to what does *faith* refer in the New Testament?

Prayer Focus

*Ask God to help you be strong in all five aspects (humility, gentleness, patience, forbearance, unity) of the worthy walk. Spend some extra time in prayer for the one or two characteristics you are most weak in.

*Thank the Lord for the teaching you have received at your church and in other contexts where you have studied the Word and doctrine. Pray that He would keep your desire strong for knowing and applying the truth.

Optional Activities

1. If you know a new Christian or a friend who's been a believer for a while but is not solidly grounded in good teaching, write him/her a letter of instruction or encouragement, based on what you've learned from this chapter. You could simply summarize and outline the main points and direct them to several important verses that chapter 5 quotes.

2. Select one or two basic Christian doctrines for more in-depth study. Perhaps they would be ones you need a better grasp on. Try to use a handbook that is thorough and yet readable, such as *Know the Truth* by Bruce Milne (Downers Grove, Ill.: InterVarsity, 1982) or *The Moody Handbook of Theology* by Paul Enns (Chicago: Moody, 1989).

Assignment

1. Read Acts 15. How did the Holy Spirit guide the church through a difficult issue? How did the members at the council display spiritual maturity?

2. Read chapter 6 of *The Body Dynamic*.

6
Building Up the Body

Session Topic
God gives each local church gifted leaders to teach and equip believers for the exercise of their spiritual gifts and the building up of others within the Body.

Community Builder *(Choose One)*
1. Have you ever felt burned out regarding your job (past or present) or a ministry in your church? Do you think burnout can be avoided? What are some practical ways?
2. Some people will tell you, "Just leave it to the experts," but others will caution, "You can't trust the experts." Which way do you tend to lean in your personal and business dealings? Why?

Group Discovery Questions
1. Are the gifts mentioned in Ephesians 4:11-12 the same as general spiritual gifts? If not, how do they differ?
2. What truth did the apostles teach (what did it become synonymous with)? How did God authenticate the teaching?
3. What was the potential problem posed by the prophetic role? Is it something we still need to be concerned about today?
4. How do some churches and denominations miss the definition of evangelist when they send men out in that capacity?
5. What is the pastor-teacher's main task?
6. Who is to have the primary responsibility for order in the local church? What can happen when an assembly does not follow Scripture concerning this matter?
7. What must be taught month in and month out in the local gathering of Christ's Body? What difference will it make in believers' lives if such teaching is not emphasized?
8. Is there a proper place for the modern division between clergy and laity in the church? Does what happened in Acts 6:1-6 align with your answer? Explain.

9. What kind of cycle should every congregation be involved in? What will such a process continually be producing? How was Philip an example?

10. List and comment briefly on each of the five results of the spiritual maturation process (Eph. 4:13-15).

Prayer Focus

*Ask the Lord to help you be more committed than ever to making progress toward spiritual maturity.

*Pray that your pastor would stay focused on his main task, "the equipping of the saints" (Eph. 4:12).

*Thank God for the specific ministry He has given you in your local church. If you do not have one at this time, ask Him to direct you to the right place of service.

Optional Activities

1. Using both your Bible and a Bible handbook, dictionary, or encyclopedia, do a short character study of Epaphras. Record the most notable character qualities you see in him. Which one stands out as most significant?

2. Read and study Acts 20:17-38. How is Paul's statement in verse 27 demonstrated elsewhere in this passage? In other places in his epistles? Record the different aspects of Paul's ministry and message found in these other references. (You will probably need a concordance for this exercise.)

Assignment

1. Memorize Ephesians 4:15-16.

2. Read chapter 7 of *The Body Dynamic.*

7
The Unity of the Body

Session Topic
All members of the Body of Christ are one in the Holy Spirit, yet they exercise a diversity of gifts.

Community Builder (*Choose One*)
1. We're all knowledgeable or skilled in at least one area. But no matter how many fields of expertise we might have, there often seems to be one extra thing we wish we were good at. Name one of those "if onlys" and say why you chose it.
2. Today's society seems to be marked by more and more disunity and fragmentation. Many factors (family breakdown, materialism, crime, racism, etc.) have been blamed for this trend. If you had the power to do so, which one of those causes (or another one) would you eliminate first? Why?

Group Discovery Questions
1. What part of the physical body is Christ equated with in the analogy of His spiritual Body, the church? Why is this part the most crucial one?
2. Do Christians naturally show forth their oneness? If not, what is the tendency, and what does that mean for pastors?
3. What does the Greek word *ekklesia* mean? What does this imply regarding the purpose of the church?
4. What is one prominent, man-made barrier within the Body that Christ has removed?
5. What virtue is equated with the mind of Christ? (see Phil. 2:6-8)
6. Evaluate the statement "I love that person in the Lord." Is it a biblical expression? What true emotion does it often cloak?
7. What quality in addition to unity is necessary for the Body to function properly? (1 Cor. 12:6, 11, 14)

Prayer Focus
*Ask the Lord to give you a firm commitment to promote unity within your local church.
*If you know of a situation in which two or more believers are at odds with one another, pray that God's peace and harmony would be restored.

Optional Activities
1. Read through John 17 at least three times each week for the next month. Read this chapter in several modern translations. Meditate on the rich truths of Jesus' prayer and write down your thoughts and insights. Select two or three key verses to memorize.
2. Take some time in the coming weeks to minister in ways that would strengthen the oneness between you and others in your church. Keep track of how those efforts turn out and record some lessons God teaches you. Thank Him for whatever results, even if it seems small to you.

Assignment
1. Memorize 1 Corinthians 12:12 or Philippians 2:1-4.
2. Read chapter 8 of *The Body Dynamic*.

8
The Gifts of the Body

Session Topic
God has given every member of Christ's Body a spiritual gift so that each believer may minister to fellow believers within the Body and the entire Body may reflect Christ's character to the world.

Community Builder *(Choose One)*
1. From time to time many of us wish we possessed a certain spiritual gift that we don't have. Which one have you imagined yourself having? How could you see that gift improving your ministry?
2. Other than preaching and teaching, what particular spiritual gift from another believer made a great impact on you in the past? Share briefly why it had such a profound effect. (This may have been something that happened just once or many times.)

Group Discovery Questions
1. Name a couple of reasons that the early church (in Acts) was so exciting. How could today's church profit from being more like the earliest one in Jerusalem?
2. What is the definition of a spiritual gift? Who is the source? How widely distributed are the gifts?
3. Give an example of a natural ability. How does this differ from a spiritual gift?
4. Does possessing a spiritual gift guarantee that it will be used? Why or why not?
5. What are three basic steps that will ensure usefulness for a spiritual gift?
6. How do temporary gifts differ from permanent ones?
7. What is the definition of prophecy? How has this changed from Old Testament times? Is there still the office of prophet?
8. How is preaching related to prophecy? What is the importance of preaching for the Body today?
9. How would you define the gift of teaching? Does this gift need

to be exercised in a formal church setting to be valid?

10. Compare and contrast the gifts of wisdom and knowledge. What part does one's intellectual capacity play in the possession and exercise of these gifts?

11. List and define the three "love gifts."

Prayer Focus

*Praise and thank God that He has given such a variety of spiritual gifts to build up the church.

*If you know what your gift is, thank God for it and ask Him to help you be faithful as you continue to serve Him with it. If you're not sure about your gift, pray that the Lord would reveal it to you through His Word (see Rom. 12:3-8 and 1 Cor. 12:1-11).

Optional Activities

1. Go to your local Christian bookstore or your church library and obtain a good biography of a notable Christian leader from the past (e.g., John Wesley, George Whitefield, Hudson Taylor, Charles Spurgeon). As you read the book, pay special attention to how the person used his spiritual gift. Ask God to help you glean some lessons that would apply to your Christian life.

2. We have seen in this chapter that whenever a believer uses his spiritual gift it must be done in love. Reread the well-known chapter on love, 1 Corinthians 13. What specific characteristics of love does the chapter mention? Spend some extra time meditating on the entire chapter. You may want to copy out a verse or two to memorize or carry with you as a reminder.

Assignment

1. Memorize Romans 12:1-2 or Ephesians 6:18.

2. Read chapter 9 of *The Body Dynamic*.

9
The Fellowship of the Body

Session Topic
Because God designed people for fellowship, the Body of Christ should be the epitome of genuine fellowship that results in practical unity.

Community Builder *(Choose One)*
1. Most of us have had some misunderstanding of what fellowship really is. What's the most common misconception you had about it prior to reading this chapter or doing other study on the topic?
2. Is genuine fellowship always incompatible with fun and enjoyment? Why or why not? Think of one thing you would do to make fellowship times with your group or at your church more interesting and profitable.

Group Discovery Questions
1. What does the Greek word *koinonia* mean? What basis does it provide for the church? (1 John 1:3)
2. Theologically, who is our primary fellowship with? Is this fellowship ever completely broken for the true Christian?
3. What most affects the joy of fellowship with God?
4. What elements made up the kind of fellowship enjoyed by the early Christians? Do you think any one of those elements is more essential than the others?
5. What church observance symbolizes true Body fellowship? What happened when that rite was abused in the Corinthian church?
6. Regarding sin within the Body, what two initial obligations do members have?
7. Under what general circumstances might a person in the Body need to be put out by the whole congregation?
8. What kind of love will help the Body avoid favoritism among members? (1 Peter 1:22; 1 John 4:7)
9. What three "one anothers" are presented at the end of this chap-

ter on Body fellowship? Which of those areas do you personally feel the most need to improve in?

Prayer Focus

*Thank God for each member of your study group and for the fellowship you've had through the Word.

*If you know of someone in your church who has an urgent need for money, shelter, or food, pray for that person or family. Ask the Lord what you can do in a tangible way to help meet the need, and then act accordingly.

*Pray that you would have a purer, more impartial love for everyone in your church. Confess and repent of anything that you might have done to hinder such love in the past.

Optional Activities

1. Prior to the next two or three times your church observes the Lord's Table, spend some time preparing your heart and mind. Confess your sins to God, meditate on His attributes or on the meaning of Christ's death. Read a Scripture passage on Communion, such as the familiar one in 1 Corinthians 11:20-33, or an account of Christ's suffering and death in one of the Gospels. Share with someone what God has taught you and how Communion has become more meaningful since you took additional time to prepare.

2. Do a short, but more in-depth study of Matthew 18:15-20. Read the passage in several translations and then read a sound commentary on it (such as *Matthew 16–23*, MacArthur New Testament Commentary [Chicago: Moody, 1988], 123–39). As you study, take some notes and make your own simple outline of the key truths concerning church discipline. If your church has not followed these principles, pray and seek a way that you might be an influence for the leadership to begin obeying them.

Assignment

1. Memorize John 15:26-27.
2. Read chapter 10 of *The Body Dynamic.*

10
The Witness of the Body

Session Topic
The Body of Christ, as it matures into His image, is expected to witness to the world in the power of the Holy Spirit.

Community Builder *(Choose One)*
1. Tell the other members of your group what has been the most helpful thing you've learned in this study of *The Body Dynamic*. Why or how do you think it will change your thinking or your actions?
2. Have you ever testified as a witness in a court case? What was the most memorable or challenging aspect about it? If you were a juror, what about the trial or courtroom procedures did you find most informative or significant?

Group Discovery Questions
1. What does John 15:26-27 suggest as a basic illustration or analogy for what the Body's witness is? Is that a fair representation? What role does each individual believer have?
2. What is the biblical meaning of "the world"? What is its position in relation to the Body?
3. A truly scriptural sermon or testimony is always related to whom?
4. What, with the Holy Spirit's help, was God the Father's supreme concern in witnessing?
5. In what three basic ways did God reveal who Jesus is?
6. In whom does the Holy Spirit live today? What difference does that make for the Body's witness?
7. In what two ways does the Body serve as a whole witness to the world?
8. Who are the last links in the witness of the Body? Why and how are they so crucial in God's plan?

Prayer Focus
*Thank God for His amazing plan for the Body's witness and for the resources we have to carry out the plan.

*Pray for an evangelist or missionary you know. Ask the Lord to strengthen him/her and to keep him/her as a faithful witness of Christ and His Body.

Optional Activities

1. Read J.I. Packer's book, *Evangelism and the Sovereignty of God* (Downers Grove, Ill.: InterVarsity, 1961). Have your Bible alongside as you read so that you can look up the many Scripture references the book cites. After you have finished the book, write a short paragraph to yourself that will remind you of the book's impact regarding your future witness.

2. Perhaps it has been a long time since you revised the contents of your personal testimony. Maybe you need to compose one for the very first time. Whichever the case, take whatever time necessary to review in writing what God has done in saving you. Make sure it is more than a mere spiritual autobiography, but that a listener would know how and why you reflect Christ's Body.

Assignment

1. Review the Scripture memory verses suggested in the Personal and Group Study Guide. Learn one or two you were not able to do earlier in the study.

2. Send a note to your group leader thanking him or her for faithful ministry in preparing and leading the group. Mention what you most appreciated about the entire time.

Scripture Index

Subject Index

A

Administration, gift of *111*
Admonishing. See also Burden-bearing *124*
Adoption (spiritual) *19*
Apostles (in New Testament)
    Paul's call *74*
    and problem in Acts 6 *79*
    secondary group *74*
    the Twelve *74*
    their role *74*
Aristides, on definition of church *7*
Armstrong, Louis *55*
Attributes of God, and the believer *56*

B

Baptism, ordinance of *70*
Body of Christ, oneness of *87*
Building up (with Scripture) *124*
Burden-bearing. See also Admonishing
    and confronting *122*
    and restoration *123*
    meaning of *121*

C

Cemetery illustration (World War II) *91*
Church
    to be impartial *90*
    birth of *100*
    metaphors for *8, 89*
Circus illustration *81*
Confession of sin *119*

D

"Desires" (in Ephesians 2:3), definition *42*